John Ellis Lanceley

The Virgin Mary, and other sermons

preached in the New Richmond Methodist Church, McCaul Street, Toronto

John Ellis Lanceley

The Virgin Mary, and other sermons
preached in the New Richmond Methodist Church, McCaul Street, Toronto

ISBN/EAN: 9783744745468

Printed in Europe, USA, Canada, Australia, Japan

Cover: Foto ©Lupo / pixelio.de

More available books at **www.hansebooks.com**

THE VIRGIN MARY

AND OTHER SERMONS,

Preached in the New Richmond Methodist Church, McCaul Street, Toronto,

BY

REV. JOHN ELLIS LANCELEY,

AND

PUBLISHED BY REQUEST.

TORONTO, CANADA:
WILLIAM BRIGGS,
WESLEY BUILDINGS.

C. W. COATES, MONTREAL.   S. F. HUESTIS, HALIFAX.

1891.

Entered according to the Act of the Parliament of Canada, in the year one thousand eight hundred and ninety-one, by WILLIAM BRIGGS, in the Office of the Minister of Agriculture, at Ottawa.

PREFACE.

NEW RICHMOND CHURCH, TORONTO.

These sermons are published in response to a requisition. This accounts for the appearance of the book, and for the choice of the subjects treated. It explains also their retaining the simple, unpretending style of their first delivery. No thought of publication entered into their form of preparation. They must not be read as exhaustive treatises, but as fragmentary studies. The preacher always tried to find the truth for the day and the hour—for his people. His honest effort was to find out what of the truth they had not perceived, and endeavor to set that before them. If, therefore, the general reader misses too largely the old familiar views of things, he must not think that such have been discarded in our ministry, but that they have been supple-

PREFACE.

mented. We do not discard the encyclopædia when we add the supplement.

In the infinitude of the themes of pulpit discussion there is room for all the righteous thought of man. The truth has to undergo the disadvantage of being seen and then proclaimed by limited understandings. For this reason the light of many minds is better than that of one. Realizing how helpful have been the thoughts and experiences of others to correct and direct his own mind and heart, the author has ventured to hope that some features of the Divine revelation may have been brought to view, in these preparations of thought for the study of God's children, as may be both new and true to the reader. The same prayer that accompanied their utterance in the pulpit follows them in their wider proclamation. May it please God to answer it.

J. E. L.

CONTENTS.

SECTION FIRST.

I. THE VIRGIN MARY 11

"For, behold, from henceforth all generations shall call me blessed."—LUKE i. 48.

II. THE GROWING CHRIST 29

"And Jesus increased in wisdom and stature, and in favor with God and man."—LUKE ii. 52.

III. THE WORSHIP OF THE MAGI 49

"Now when Jesus was born in Bethlehem of Judæa in the days of Herod the king, behold, there came wise men from the east to Jerusalem, saying, Where is He that is born King of the Jews? for we have seen His star in the east, and are come to worship Him. . . . And when they were come into the house, they saw the young child with Mary His mother, and fell down, and worshipped Him: and when they had opened their treasures, they presented unto Him gifts, gold, and frankincense, and myrrh."—MATTHEW ii. 1, 2, 11.

IV. THE CHRIST PROCLAIMED 69

"And Jesus answering said unto him, Suffer it to be so now: for thus it becometh us to fulfil all righteousness. . . . And Jesus, when He was baptized, went up straightway out of the water; and, lo, the heavens were opened unto Him, and He saw the Spirit of God descending like a dove, and lighting upon Him. And lo a voice from heaven, saying, This is my beloved Son, in whom I am well pleased."—MATTHEW iii. 15-17.

HYMN—"Yesterday, To-day and To-morrow" . 86

CONTENTS.

V. THE BEGINNING OF THE WORK - - - - 89
    (THE WILDERNESS AND THE DEVIL.)

"Then was Jesus led up of the spirit into the wilderness to be tempted of the devil. And when He had fasted forty days and forty nights, He was afterward an hungred. . . . And . . . the tempter came to Him. . . ."—MATTHEW iv. 1-4.

POETRY—"Life is Not in Bread" - - - - 111

VI. FORMING ATTACHMENTS - - - - - 119

"And the two disciples heard Him speak, and they followed Jesus. Then Jesus turned, and saw them following, and saith unto them, What seek ye? They said unto Him, Rabbi, Where dwellest Thou? He saith unto them, Come and see."—JOHN i. 37-39.

VII. AT THE MARRIAGE - - - - - - 141

"And the third day there was a marriage in Cana of Galilee; and the mother of Jesus was there: and both Jesus was called, and His disciples, to the marriage."—JOHN ii. 1, 2.

SECTION SECOND.

VIII. THE BIBLE AND PROHIBITION - - - - 161

"Art thou for us, or for our adversaries?"—JOSHUA v. 13.

IX. PERFECT - - - - - - - - 187

"Be ye therefore perfect, even as your Father which is in heaven is perfect."—MATTHEW v. 48

X. THE PULPIT AND SOCIAL QUESTIONS - - - 203

"The Spirit of the Lord God is upon me; because the Lord hath anointed me to preach good tidings unto the meek; He hath sent me to bind up the brokenhearted, to proclaim liberty to the captives, and the opening of the prison to them that are bound."—ISAIAH lxi. 1.

XI. THE TRUE SOLDIER - - - - - - 223
    (PREACHED TO THE QUEEN'S OWN RIFLES, TORONTO.)

"For we which live are alway delivered unto death for Jesus' sake, that the life also of Jesus might be made manifest in our mortal flesh."—II CORINTHIANS iv. 11.

CONTENTS.

XII. A Greek Proverb - - - - - - 237

"Except a corn of wheat fall into the ground and die, it abideth alone: but if it die, it bringeth forth much fruit."—John xii. 24.

XIII. The Lord's Battle - - - - - - 261

"And all this assembly shall know that the Lord saveth not with sword and spear: for the battle is the Lord's."—1 Samuel xvii. 47.

XIV. The Apocalyptic Appearance - - - - 281

"And I turned to see the voice that spake with me. And being turned, I saw seven golden candlesticks; and in the midst of the seven candlesticks one like unto the Son of man, clothed with a garment down to the foot, and girt about the paps with a golden girdle. His head and His hairs were white like wool, as white as snow; and His eyes were as a flame of fire; and His feet like unto fine brass, as if they burned in a furnace; and His voice as the sound of many waters. And He had in His right hand seven stars: and out of His mouth went a sharp twoedged sword: and His countenance was as the sun shineth in his strength. And when I saw Him I fell at His feet as dead. And He laid His right hand upon me, saying unto me, Fear not; I am the first and the last: I am He that liveth, and was dead; and, behold, I am alive for evermore, Amen; and have the keys of hell and of death. Write the things which thou hast seen, and the things which are, and the things which shall be hereafter; the mystery of the seven stars which thou sawest in My right hand, and the seven golden candlesticks. The seven stars are the angels of the seven churches: and the seven candlesticks which thou sawest are the seven churches."—Revelation i. 12-20.

I.

THE VIRGIN MARY.

"For, behold, from henceforth all generations shall call me blessed."

—Luke i. 48.

THE VIRGIN MARY.

I AM led to suppose that many of you, as lovers of the Lord Jesus, have been refreshing your memories and your hearts by reading over again during the past week the record of the Saviour's birth. The Christmas season calls us to the thought of the most marvellous of all births known to this earth. In my own review of it, as the season came, I was led to take special cognizance of His mother, and of certain great preparations which had a part in producing the world's Redeemer, and qualifying Him for His work. And really, I feel it to be right for me to confess that I have never done my honest duty to that honorable and gracious one, whose place among women is the highest in the will of God. When I examine my own heart as to how I could pass by, with such little notice, so important a character and personage as the *Virgin Mary*, the mother of Jesus, I am compelled to own that I found a prejudice deep-seated there which had robbed my mind of any interest in her. I am ashamed beyond measure, as I come face to face with the record divinely given for our edification and salvation, that I should have been so long blind to the beauty and worthiness of the one chosen of God for the mission so divine. And when I read the words of this morning's text, uttered under the sense of the divine presence and blessing, and find that the prophecy declared that "henceforth" she shall be called "blessed" by all generations, I feel guilty that my own soul has never uttered its "Amen" to the sublime "Magnificat," and never before chosen her character as a theme for study in the course of twenty years' exposition of the revealed Word and will of God. I am glad, indeed, that others have been truer than I to the sacred record, and that her place in history has not been hidden to the gaze of the mothers of earth's children, amid all their peculiar sympathies, touching the life of them who come into this world.

It is a wonderful story—that God must come and tabernacle in the flesh; but long before it came, the children of men had learned to expect it. They seemed to have given up all hope of an ordinary sin-born mortal being able to save the people; and, verily, the people needed a salvation. Outside the Jewish anticipation, there were in the far-off "East" those who were ready to see His star when it appeared, and come up to worship Him. Inside the Jewish hope, it was the secret height of womanly ambition to be the mother of the Messiah that was to come into the world.

On the reading of the story of the miraculous conception, I have no doubt at all but reason is disposed to revolt at the record, and refuse its allegiance to revelation. Somehow, the revolt is very natural. But we must not come to our conclusions too rashly. We must delay judgment till we mark the results of belief. Is such a faith destructive, or is it life-giving? Does it help, or does it hinder man? When we look at the Being that was thus born, and see His wonderful character and career, it helps reason to go back and accept the wonderful way of such a visitation. So wonderful a Being never came to this earth in the ordinary way. There is a consistency, a harmony, all through, which demands the very remarkable manner of birth.

And when we learn that the One to be "born" was One who was not to begin an existence at that point, but simply to reveal one in the human form, let us perceive that no one of us could conceive of a way more natural or reasonable.

The *will* of God, the *heart* of God, the *purpose* of God *in* and *toward* man, were all to be shown forth to man. Who could do this but just such an One as is recorded—the *Son* of God, the *offspring, outcome, fruit, life—what* you will—*of God*. The Spirit—which is the life—operated upon the organism directly, instead of indirectly (or through means), and *life* took form in which to make itself manifest. Godhead and manhood were to dwell together again. A second Adam, the Lord from Heaven, was to open the gates of Paradise, and set to work to restore its losses and reconstruct its ruins. It was necessary that a real woman should bear Him, lest we see the scene as a drama or a play, rather than a reality. Her record, as given us in the Word, is one especially human and womanly. It would spoil the effect sought to be reached to have it less or more. To make her more than a woman, belittles, rather than magnifies, the glorious mystery of "God manifest in the flesh."

And now, when we come to interest ourselves in the narrative, we see at once the fact that some one of earth's daughters must be chosen of God for this divine honor. And we may rest assured He will be ready to give it to the most worthy. The most worthy will be the most fit for such a service.

This honored maiden passed her early days quietly in the beautiful little city of Nazareth. Her home was a garden of flowers, on a hill top, where the air was pure and bracing, and fragrant from the breathing plants, and full of song from the trill of a thousand birds. All travellers report the same description of Nazareth as the spot more haunted by lovely flora than any spot in Palestine. Luke tells us that the maiden's name was Mary. Tradition would tell us that she was the daughter of one Joachim, a Galilean, and Anna, a native of Bethlehem; that she was the child of their old age, and that as such she was dedicated to the special service of God. Be this as it may, she was a pure young woman, who knew an angel's voice when she heard one, and was ready to obey it, too. There are angel voices always ready to lead pure hearts to holy elevations, but it seems now our maiden hearts too early soil with earthly vanity and inordinate affection to know an angel's whisper when it comes. The chapter before us says that the angel Gabriel came to her and hailed her, saying, "Thou art highly favored, the Lord is with thee." Quieting her consternation, he met her perplexity by explaining to her that she had found favor with God and should be the mother of the Messiah, who should "sit upon the throne of His father David," and should "reign for ever and ever."

She was thus called to the highest honor, and yet the most awful charge ever laid upon a mortal creature. The highest honors always carry the weightiest responsibilities. It would be idle surmising for us to try and imagine what a state the soul of Mary was in when she heard of the place she was to fill in the eternal plan. She received the tidings properly, we may depend upon that; for she was God's choice, and He would not err. For this very reason we ought to study her with the deepest love and care. How God must have loved her, to make her the mother of His Son! She was in love at the time. She was espoused to a young man named Joseph, and was just standing on the threshold of a new life, when, if ever, the heart flutters on wings of hope and fear, and excited words can easily reach the lips; but her very love was permeated with her simple trust, and was modified thereby. She must have thought of Joseph; but she trusted him, and somehow she expected to be trusted in return. If God trusted her, why should not man? Somehow, I do not think she ever knew that Joseph doubted her. The angel made that right, and did not fail to shield her from the scorn and coldness that must otherwise have wounded her. But the world—ah, they will jeer and scoff in their ignorance of the glory that is concealed in the garments of humiliation. She must bear the reproach, if she would bear the glory. Oh, yes; and how all this prepared her to be the mother of Him who, through the deepest degradation, **is to reach the** loftiest height of honor and power and glory!

The words of our text form part of a response which she gave to her cousin Elizabeth, who was just waiting the time of the birth of her own divinely promised son.

Mary, full of the thoughts which thrilled her as she pondered over the angel's message, full of the eagerness of friendship and sympathy, rose and went to the hill country to see Elizabeth. As she entered the house, her cousin, "full of the Holy Ghost," saluted her in almost the same words as the angel. Now, it had become very real. No human voice had spoken to her before of it, nor had the secret ever crossed her own lips, but now, another knew it, and she could speak of it. How natural then that what had been pondered so long in the heart, should have been stirred to the uttermost by the touch of human and womanly sympathy, and burst out into song of joy and exultation, "My soul doth magnify the Lord, and my spirit hath rejoiced in God my Saviour." This is true to nature—to human nature as we know it, too.

It seems to me that as this ejaculation of praise was so heartfelt and full, it is a good place to look for those phases of character in Mary which we ought to study, so that we may measure somewhat her influence over the Holy Child and His career; and that we may learn what kind of a *mother* God thinks it best to place over His children. For we must not suppose for a moment that Jesus was uninfluenced by His mother. If the Christ could be *born* of a woman, surely He could be nurtured and developed, loved and taught by one, without any incompatibility. And she was *fit* to teach Him; *fit* to *teach*, because willing to *learn*, and because fond of the things of which He should be fond. Fit to teach, I said; yes, *fit* because *fitted*. When she was the simple maiden Mary she lived the simplest, best and purest life she knew. And when the angel came and offered her the honor of being the mother for God, she accepted the honor and the responsibility, and consecrated herself fully to His service, saying, "Behold the handmaid of the Lord, be it unto me according to thy word." And part of the word was, "The Holy Ghost shall come upon thee." This is qualification enough to make her a teacher under God of the things concerning which they were now of one mind and heart. *Fit to teach*, I said. Yes, for we find that she had not been a dunce in the school of her day. She had a good knowledge of the history of her own people. Her very Magnificat was like a quotation of old Scripture passages. Let any one compare the utterances of old Hannah when her child Samuel was born, with those of Mary at this time, and they will feel that it is easy to see how the one gave color and tone to the other. *Fit to teach*, *yes;* for she had the *spirit* to teach a Saviour. She longed for

THE VIRGIN MARY.

the redemption of her own people. She sang in her present inspiration the song of prophecy. She saw and felt in her own son the "help of Israel," the "mercy of God," as He spake unto the fathers "*to Abraham* and his seed for *ever.*" Well might she exult, then, in such words as our text, "From henceforth all nations shall call me blessed." She rejoiced in that she was to be of service to her race. In blessing others she would herself be called "blessed." It was her very ideal of honor, to be made a medium of blessing to the needy—yea, even to a needy nation and a needy world. Her *heart* was glad, not her *head.* She was not puffed up. She sought no worship or adulation such as is vainly bestowed upon her by those who lift her level with her Divine Son. I like how Mrs. Browning here describes her:

"I am not proud—*not proud,*
　Albeit in my flesh God sent His Son,
　Albeit over Him my head is bowed
　As others bow before Him, still my heart
　Bows lower than their knees. O centuries
　That roll, in vision, your futurities
　My future grave athwart—
　Whose murmurs seem to reach me while I keep
　Watch o'er His sleep—
　Say of me as the heavenly said, 'Thou art
　The blessedest of women!'—blessedest,
　Not holiest, not noblest—no high name,
　Whose height misplaced may pierce me like a shame
　When I sit meek in heaven."

To the pure and simple woman-heart honor is always a surprise. Mary never dreamed of the blessedness to come upon her or the honor she should hold within the world. And it is upon such souls that true honor best holds its seat. It is indeed into such souls the Holy Spirit comes and the Saviour is *reborn* for men. *Reborn*, I say; for not another *Christ* will ever spring from these means, but *Christians* will, and next to the blessedness of bearing the *Christ* is the blessedness of bearing the children of the Highest, and the joint *heirs* with Jesus Christ.

How I wish we had more of this excellence—this simple unconsciousness—now! Our miscalled education is how can a young girl make a good figure in society; and it ruins the innocence of earlier years. There are so many nowadays who have never had a real childhood, never been unconscious, who possess already the thoughts and airs of womanhood, and who are applauded as objects to admire, instead of being pitied as victims of an unnatural training. Their manners, conversations, attitudes, are all *art*. Already they tremble, as we do, for the verdict of the world. Oh, it is miserable to see how we actually work to root out of our children the beauty of the virgin's early life—the beauty of unconsciousness of self.

And so when Mary received her great honor, she

felt that it was all bestowed upon her. She had no thought of having merited any of it. She was not touched by any vanity. It was all of God. "He that is mighty hath magnified me, and holy is His name." She did not say that she was unworthy, or that she felt her unworthiness. She did not feel herself, either worthy or unworthy, and so she did not speak of how she felt about herself. She was "magnifying the Lord." Oh, do you see the difference between *her* and that mock modesty, that bastard humility which trumpets its own unworthiness before every company, till all the world knows it wants to be honored for it. May we all learn to-day the sweetness, beauty, divineness of Mary's humility, even in her praises— "My soul doth magnify the Lord." She was really nothing; God was all.

But she did not fail to appreciate the great responsibility that came with the honor of her charge. She would know that if she did not the will of God who had chosen her, His glory would be marred in her unfaithfulness. She knew, somehow, that great things would be expected of her, because the Lord God had chosen her, had chosen her to bless the nation, to bless the nation through motherhood, and all its concomitants of duty and devotion.

This was true womanhood, as God chose it to nurture and qualify His Son. There is a glory for womanhood which she has never fully appreciated. There is a glory for manhood which can never be known till woman's sphere in God's service is found and filled. Woman must have a conscious relation to the dignity and glory of God's plans and purposes in this world. She must have an aspiration and an ideal in which her pure heart takes holy delight. She has a spiritual realm of special service, just as she has a natural one of natural service. There is no life known in its divine manifestation about us but has its dual unfolding. Woman must learn what is divine womanhood, and then and there she will find the human.

We refer again to Mary's joy, in that she was to be a blessing to generations. Her joy was that she was going to be an honored *woman*. She was not going to be a *man*. *Man* seemed to be laden with honors and offices of all kinds in the service of God and the temple, and woman's place seemed narrow and unhonored, indeed, at times. But womanhood was to be crowned with its own glory in her. She was not going to be given a man's sphere. She was not even going to be a *queen* upon an ivory throne, or rule society from a palace seat. But *she* would give the world a *man*, and teach him love for his people and for his race. She will see that he knows his place in life and fills it well. Her joy shall be in watching him go forth and do it. Her fulness shall be fulfilled in him. Her glory shall be seen in him. There is no glory beyond that. It is God's true glory for a woman. There is something very remarkable in the facts of history about the mothers of great men. I cannot elaborate it now. But men in whom the mother-element is strong are always benefactors of the race. They live to bless. Christ was born of *God* and a *woman*. It is more *woman* and less *man* we want in this world to-day. We have too much of the *lordly* element, and not enough of the *lady-like*. It is not more man in woman, but more woman in man, that is needed to lift up the world in the arms of love. The world wants a motherhood to nurse it, and tend it, and plead for it as only motherhood can do. Man has crushed, enslaved, belittled, conquered woman. Her nature is one that can be crushed. Woman is a tender plant; lovely, indeed, to look upon, and in her crushed condition illustrating the sentiment of the poet when he writes:

> "But Thou wilt heal the broken hearts
> Which, like the plants that throw
> Their fragrance from the wounded part,
> Breathe sweetness out of woe."

And she is verily a plant, the leaves of which are for the healing of the nations; but the secret of her healing powers will be found in the divine qualities of her motherhood. Woman can never win her way to divinely ordained eminence, by wearing man's armor or using the weapons of his warfare. She will succeed by learning lessons of Mary. Mary is not to be worshipped as a God; but she is to be studied and emulated as a woman—as *the* woman.

No one can sensibly belittle the woman power of this age, and, indeed, of all ages. Such is its natural influence that she has almost always been deified as holding the destinies of nations in her hands.

And there is no sadder sight to see than fallen woman; no uglier business than to see women misusing their influence over men. It is a pity to see them leading the men whom they could guide into high thought and active sacrifice, into the petty gossip of twaddling conversation, or into discussion of dangerous and unhealthy feeling. To see them becoming what men—in frivolous moments—wish them to be; rather than moulding men, in those weak times, into what they should be; not protesting against impurity, intemperance, unbelief, but rather giving them an underhand encouragement. Ill indeed it is, to see them turning away from their mission to bless, and exalt, and console, that they may wriggle through a thousand meannesses into some higher social position and waste their God-given energy to win precedence over a rival, spending all their neurotic force in miserable excitements with an awful and pitiable degradation; exhausting life in pleasures which fritter away and debase their character; seeking only wealth; and content only to be lapped in the folds of a silken and easy life, *unthinking* of the thousands of sisters weeping in the night for hunger and misery of heart.

Alas! Woman may say this is not her work; but if her heart be hard, depend upon it man's heart will never soften. The world wants mothers; mothers like Mary, who think it an honor to be such, and then set themselves to fill up the measure of duty and responsibility. If we had more mothers like Mary, we would have more children like Christ. Men must be *born* better before the world advances much in its heart. A purer parentage, with purer motives in parental honor and responsibility, will be the world's new blessing.

Let me urge you all to ponder the lessons of this hour. Oh! women of to-day, open your hearts unto God. Be pure, and sweet, and holy, and the angel voices will not be strange to your ears. God has messages for you that *men* can never tell. Consecrate your nature in its *own*-ness to him, and God will verily honor you. He will give you to know that you can lead the men of this country and this age to be pure and true, just and brave, loving and wise, if *you only will*. Man cannot, will not, live alone; and God has given it to woman to reign over him, if she will, by sympathy, and love, and purity. But if she fail before him, both fall degraded, till in a virgin's heart again a Christ is born and unfolded to the gaze of men to win them from their sins to purity like His, and manliness their nature longs to know.

Woman, look at the needs of the world and of the Church to-day! Comprehend it as the world's mother should. Be true to your high calling in God *now*, and "*henceforth* all generations shall call you blessed." Amen.

II.

THE GROWING CHRIST.

"And Jesus increased in wisdom and stature, and in favor with God and man."

—LUKE ii. 52.

THE GROWING CHRIST.

IN harmony with the thought of the season of the year, we were found studying last Sabbath some of the surroundings incident to the advent of the world's Redeemer. Especially we gave our attention to the mother of Jesus, and we strove to learn from the character of Mary what kind of a woman God chooses to bring into the world His anointed ones. We only found time to say a passing word on her influence over His boyhood life and her relation to His after character and qualifications for His work of redemption. The interest which was aroused over the theme of last Sabbath was to myself a pleasing surprise. The request of more than one or two of those present for the notes of the address, that they might preserve them, made me feel that there was more interest in the theme than in the preacher; and you know that is, after all, the most effective form of interest.

Can this interest be kept up? Oh! it will be

the life of our souls if we can love the truth of God's revelation. "This is life eternal to know God and Jesus Christ whom He hath sent."

In coming to the special study of to-day, I confess to you that it is almost provoking to our forms of thought and our subjects of interest in this day, that there is so little written for us about the early life of Jesus Christ.

It seems at first a little strange that the early events of the birth and childhood should have so little notice from His biographers. Matthew has but one slight reference to the mother before the birth of Jesus. Mark has nothing at all to say; and John, the beloved, has even passed by the testimony of the early years. This very silence of the others makes us turn with interest increased to the one who speaks. The private address of Luke's gospel seems to indicate that the writer had a very strong personal interest in the writing of it. He was evidently intense in his devotion to the actual history of Jesus. He has, therefore, gone into details upon what to him were points of importance and interest unsought for by the others. And indeed, if we look closely into this matter, we will see that the facts here narrated are not very easy to get. Where, think you, did the writer go for his information? Is it not *mothers* who supply all the stories of their children's infant years? And does not this fact prompt us by its very naturalness to the source of knowledge. Indeed, as we sit and read it, do we not find the whole coloring of the narrative altogether feminine. The memories are those of a woman, and there is such a sweet gracefulness, and holy solemnity, and tender lovableness about them all as to suggest to us at once the pure heart of the virgin who sang the hymn of joy we pondered last Sabbath—the mother whose heart, long ere this record was written, a sword had pierced. But why should Luke, and not Matthew, Mark or John, have gathered this information? There is a peculiar interest here. I have never found it referred to among the students of apologetics, but to me it is very significant. Who should be as well qualified by interest and by propriety to *gather* these details and *sift* them, and afterwards *record* them to the world, as he whose profession was that of "the beloved physician." Our physicians are usually the greatest dogmatists of doubt on the whole question of the incarnation; and there is a peculiar fitness all round, it seems to me, in the divine choice of a physician to speak these marvellous words to the wondering children of men.

But even with Luke's valuable addition, the story of the early life of Jesus is sparsely told. We need not, however, be surprised at this; for readers of history will tell us that it was not customary in those days to write much about infants or little children. The early years were considered too commonplace to be worthy of notice. Childhood was not respected then as it is now. We have no histories of any of the great ones—Cæsar, Virgil, Cicero, and the like—till they began their active years of service. It is different now. We look at youth as a great cause, whose effect will appear in age. We feel that in this fact lies our hope and our responsibility toward all social reform. And this consideration is happily increasing with us. I remember some years ago startling a large Sunday-school of teachers and scholars, by asserting that the Bible did not record a good man who was not always good, or who was not a good child. There seemed to be a dissent quite widespread among the listeners, till I asked for a hand uplifted by any one who could tell me of a Bible *good man* that was a *bad boy*. When the test was put, and no answer given, it set them to think more seriously upon that worthy study of our age—the value of youth.

And so it is, I infer, that we come with more of interest than any former age to study the early years of Jesus, and feel sorry that more has not been recorded for our consideration. There is sufficient here, however, to show us that He passed through all the necessary developments incident to the childhood of a human life;

that He had to learn truth as all others have to learn it, and that He was blessed in having so holy and helpful and teachable a mother. I say *teachable*, for only the teachable can teach. And one needs to be very teachable—very ready to learn from the unfolding nature we seek to train. The brief record which Matthew gives us of the first two years of the young life, reveals to us that they were years when the mother had much to learn concerning her son. She was called to wonder and joy mingled, when she found that wise men from the far away East came by the guidance of a star to worship Him and present their gifts of homage to Him. But she had only just been given this thrill of joy, when she must be summoned to pack up and flee into the distant Egypt, for Herod the King sought the young child's life to take it away. She was the guardian of the child's physical life, under the eye of heaven. But His safety depended upon the obedience of the mother to the voice that came in the dream, or in the vision of the night. And surely we may somewhat conceive the intensity of solemn responsibility which she must have developed, when she felt, as she looked into His little noticing eyes, that there were foes alert to destroy Him, and the sword already pierces her heart at the thought of having to protect Him from the sword of kings; and then to prove a worthy mother for such a possible child.

And there is no difference in kind between this and the interest which all true motherhood feels toward its offspring born into a possible heirship to the same throne, as joint occupants with Him whose life we find so interesting. The safety of every child is in the mother's keeping. The kings of this world seek every child's life to destroy it, while the messages of God come to all our little ones, since Jesus in His maturity said, "Suffer the little ones to come unto Me, and forbid them not, for of such is the kingdom of heaven."

The next record of the sacred writers is when at twelve years of age he visited Jerusalem at the passover feast with His mother and Joseph. Whether He had ever been before is not recorded, but we may not do anything else but believe that the story of the passover angel in Egypt had been told over and over again to His listening ears and heart. And now He was going up with His parents to attend what they had always attended with solemn import each year of His growing life. In great companies the people from all Palestine journeyed at this time to the holy city, singing Psalms ofttimes along the way. It would have been a solemn charm to the earnest boy to hear them, as the hills of Zion rose to view before their near approach to Jerusalem, strike up the cymbal and the song in David's words, "I will lift up mine eyes unto the hills, from whence cometh my help." And what real power would the passover service have over his soul! It would mean all it could to Him. When the lamb was slain He would see the blood gushing into the golden cup and thrown at the foot of the altar of burnt offering. And the burden of human sin would touch His tender heart then. And when the supper came, and the *ten*, at the least, must be present, and the youngest in the company must ask, when the second wine-cup was filled, "What mean ye by this service?" is it not reasonable to think that He, the *youthful Jesus*, should be the One to ask this question, and hear the rehearsal once more from the head of the company, of all the story of Egypt and emancipation—the story of Israel's first *redemption*. His divinely chosen mother had not failed to make His heart susceptible to all these things; and she would watch with eager interest His first association with these significant types and symbols.

The feast lasted about a week, and after it was over the companies would prepare at once for their homeward march. The Nazareth caravan started on its way, and, as the record reads to us, there came a three days' loss of the "mother's holy child." Again we may readily believe the "sword" entered her heart; and I have wondered if this three days' loss was only a forecast, or perhaps a *foretaste*, of the other *three days' loss* that came in the last days of His earthly career when the sword pierced through her heart, as she watched the sad scenes of Golgotha, and wept as He gave up the ghost. But a search for Him resulted in His being found in the temple, where the teachers were reading and expounding the law in its literalness. And the record leads us to think that His questions, and even His answers, were remarkable indeed. They would be. What truly spiritual conceptions of the truth did those Scribes and Elders possess anyway? They never seemed to know the meanings of the sayings of the Holy Ghost by the prophets.

To a child all things are simple and all things are pure. The young Jesus might easily ask questions, and give answers, too, that would embarrass any Priest or Levite or Scribe who knew only the letter of the law, and saw no hope, only in the human arm of some coming king of common earthly potentiality. Had not His mother taught him that to be *good* was to be *great?* Had not His mother told Him that God's ways were not the ways of men? Had not the old victories been of weakness over strength, of David over Goliath, of meekness over pride? Had He not probably heard the words of the old prophet, "Not by might nor by power, but by My Spirit, saith the Lord of Hosts." If, then, in questioning the Rabbi of the meaning of the words, as well as of the symbols in which they had lately been engaged, the coming Messiah should be spoken of as one of earthly pomp and prestige; could He not ask, "How can a big king make people good?" That would puzzle a literalist; and yet a child would easily ask it. I think we must seek for the naturalness of all this development, and not seek to un-*man* Him, who specially *manned* Himself for this gracious work of redemption.

But His parents are seeking Him. They are in trouble, nay, they have just found Him here. And they ask Him the why of this absence. And the answer comes so simple and so natural, "Wist ye not that I must be about *My* father's business." As it reads here so plain and unqualified, yet in a vernacular not quite home-like to us, it does not leave upon us the correct impression. It was not wonderful that the boy of Mary should want to see the temple—the house of God—the working place of the kingdom. If He had been there for a few moments at some other time during the feast, he would be sure to desire to hear a service, or to converse with the holy men who waited at its courts. We have seen our own boys stand about an interested spot, and not rest satisfied till they had asked some question of the keeper concerning the things that had stirred up heir interest. The temple was His home. His own mother had told him that God was *His* Father; and this was then *His* Father's house—yes, I was going to say *His* Father's "*shop*," and all this service was *His* Father's business.

His earthly foster-father had a house, and a shop, and a business, and he had always found some interest there. But when His mother called His attention to those again as His place, He couldn't help saying to her who had taught Him: "You say that you and My father have sought Me sorrowing. Oh, mother, is not God My Father, is not this His house—My home, is not this His business, and should I not learn to work here?" "Wist ye not!" *i.e.*, "Do you not know, mother, that I ought to be here?" Was not He stating only His own first inpulse of correspondencies, and asking His mother's advice?

But God led Mary to take Him home and let Him learn subjection. It is said He went with them and became "subject unto them." Certainly, "subject!" it is the only way to know how to rule. He obeyed, and so learned what obedience was before He should exact it of others. He proved the value of such a discipline before He went to put it before His own disciples. He went home to Nazareth and lived that life which all boys have to live; the hardest life in some ways that we have, when we are to do only what we are told, often not knowing the *why*, save that it is our father's or mother's will. "Thus it became Him to fulfil all righteousness," that is, to *do all things that are right.* How could He teach, "Children obey your parents in the Lord," if He obeyed not His own? "I am among you as He that serveth" were His words unto His own disciples. So could He teach that by faithful service does one save his life, even the life thus given away.

So now He is at home in Nazareth; and we hear not of Him again till He comes forth as the divine Son upon whom the Spirit descends as a dove, and whom John announces as the Lamb of God, which taketh away the sin of the world. But a long time has elapsed between these points of history. Eighteen years without a record. Was it uneventful? Well, yes, and yet no. It was eventful—full of events—and these events form habits—habits of thought, and word, and deed. Do you ask the occupancy of these important years? I think we can best judge them by their fruit. Evidently we can reasonably infer the interim from the two extremes. At twelve we find Him with certain tastes and tendencies, and afterward He comes to the front a skilled and perfect example of His earlier aims and hopes. If we should find a boy of twelve years making good figures upon a slate and sketching with youthful interest upon the drawing-book, and then, having disappeared for years, he should suddenly come back to view as a skilled artist making beautiful pictures, we should know that the meantime had been spent in continuation of what we saw at twelve. If Achilles chose a sword when a child, and then in mature life waked up the troops upon many a battle-field, we must conclude that all through and through he was a soldier from heart to brain, from head to foot. And so in this great world of analogies, we see Jesus at the age of twelve studying the great questions of man's life, and thinking of His business as that between God and men ; and lo, when He enters life's great arena He comes with healing for men's woes and wisdom for men's wants, and the Sermon on the Mount upon His lips; and we guess—nay, we know, that the eighteen unseen years, He was working up and putting into conscious experience those truths which afterward shone like a sunlight upon a darkened world.

He lived the ordinary human life. That was probably the hardest thing for Him to do. Doubtless there was a potent tendency to do unusual things; but He was restrained. To me His doing nothing wonderful, was the wonderful thing. I believe He gained His strength for His wilderness temptation by the habits of His subjection to ordinary habits of life. Moreover, when we find Him called the carpenter's Son, and know that He spent His days of toil with His father, Joseph, we can see Him a servant in His father's employ. But thus He dignified labor, and showed that a man could work at a trade from daylight till dark and prepare his mind with truth and his heart with devotion enough to enlighten and save the *world*. I see Him, I think, at the honorable toil of *making things*. Yes; of *making useful* things, ploughs and carts and such like, for those who planted and sowed the fields and sought the redemption of the ground. He *served*, served His day and generation, earned His living, won His life, *made* a living, as we say; and then, having *won* it and *possessed* it as a *human right*, went out and laid it down for men. And when He came forth, the people knew Him as that "Son of the Carpenter;" and here was the mystery—and yet the glory—that He should be able to do it.

The time passes rapidly, but I want to note that while a great work evidently went on during those eighteen years, it went on silently. All the great works of God grow in silence. Men in their clumsy work make a noise.

Remember how it was said of the temple when it was building: "There was neither hammer, nor axe, nor any tool of iron heard in the house while it was in building." Jesus grew as the temple grew, in the silence of fitted stones. We could all learn a lesson here. If we are to grow in grace to a power of usefulness to come, we ought to have a good long silent season. If the Church is to grow, it is not to be by boasting and contention, but by quietly drinking in the light of the face of God.

I tell you to-day, in the presence of this study of truth, that in the glaring publicity given to the affairs of Churches, the parades of statistics and clatter of machinery, there cannot be much true growth. When we hear loud noise and ostentatious boasting and elaborate advertisement, we may just remember that "the kingdom of God cometh not with observation;" and for the most part true progress does not come in that way. Hankerings after great demonstrations, to which we know the world will turn its eyes, show a misapprehension of true life. And what is true about a Church, is true about an individual. You know—I know—that our drinking in of Christ's Spirit, our risings in the life of God, never came to us in our seasons of boasting or of publicity, but in our unostentatious quiet of ordinary honorable duty and prayer.

There is one more point of interest that some of you may have thought about. Why was not Jesus brought up at Jerusalem? Why not allowed all the great privileges of the holy city of Jerusalem? Why not the fellowship of its priests and rulers and rabbis?

How shall we answer that question? We see that when He reached His maturity and came to Jerusalem, He was entirely out of sympathy with the spirit and manner of its officers. Death was to be their treatment of Him. We can see that His teaching was quite heretical from their standpoint, and they felt that His preaching would ruin the Church. There must have been some design in all this. Evidently He was to be a rebuke to them for their errors. They had grown narrow and exclusive in their spirit, and so unfit to lead the world to God, its Father. Somehow, then, there was a reason for His being sent to live His preparatory life in "Galilee of the Gentiles." He was to break down this wall of partition that had been built up between them. It was, you will recollect, a reproach to Christ that He was a Galilean, and it was asked, sneeringly, "Can any good come out of Nazareth?" But by whom was this question inspired? Evidently the strict, narrow, bigoted Jerusalem Jews. Galilee was outside the charmed circle of Jewish orthodoxy. And the early education was not to be where the worship of Mosaic literalisms was so unbending. His early associates were not only of the Jewish cast of mind; and among His disciples was found Philip, of Bethsaida, to whom the Greeks could familiarly come, saying, "*We* would see Jesus." So that Galilee, which won for Him the reproach of Jerusalem, did, at the same time, help Him to win the esteem of the human race; for in Galilee the fetters of Mosaism had become so weakened that they did not bind the soul who wanted to speak such thoughts as He came forth to utter in His broad sayings to the woman of Samaria, and to the inquiring Greeks, and to all of mankind in His Sermon on the Mount. And so we find that when the inscription was written upon the cross of the crucified, it was not written for a class, but for all classes, in Hebrew and Greek and Latin, for Jew, and Greek, and Roman, to ponder and to be effected thereby.

I feel sorry that our time will not permit any further study of this profitable theme just now. How little we thought there was to be learned from the meditation of the childhood of Jesus. O wonderful child! Set, indeed, for the fall and the rising of the world. Thy childhood is a mystery to be unfolded. Did the Great Infinite fold Himself in such a span? Thoughts look out to us as indeed from Thy sacred enclosure, which we are unable to utter. The Word was made flesh and dwelt among us, full of grace and truth. "When Thou tookest upon Thyself to deliver man, Thou didst not abhor the virgin's womb." And Thou didst become the child to say to us by that subjection, "Except a man become as a little child he cannot enter into the kingdom of heaven." Oh, how we see how "Thou hast chosen the weak things of this world to confound the things that are mighty." Jesus in the arms of Mary, Jesus an infant, Jesus a child. All earth and hell seeking to destroy, and all salvation safely folded in those beautiful baby hands. "Out of the mouth of babes and sucklings Thou hast perfected praise, that Thou mightest still the enemy and the avenger."

And when we mark childhood so consecrated, is it not dreadful to see Christ's image defaced in the degradation of childhood. Is it not pitiful to behold in our streets and lanes, faces and eyes that have a primeval sweetness in them, reminding us of His, but hardening daily before us into sin and shame. Look at those children upon our highway! What separates them from heaven? See that little face—a real sweetness beneath all that stain! Why don't we sigh and wonder? Oh, holy child Jesus! in our day rise up for the children! Hear Mrs. Browning's plea: "Do ye not hear the children crying, oh, my brothers," from factory, and city, and street, and gaol? Our children are crushed beneath the great Juggernaut of this materialistic civilization of our time, intemperance and greed of gain, and the endless mockeries and frivolities of our fashionable ways. Oh, holy child Jesus, rise up for the children !

My dear brothers and sisters in the Lord Christ, let us learn to-day the sanctity of childhood. Let us seek by all true means to make the children temples of the mind of the Holy Child. Let our study of the mother and child bring us its beautiful lessons to parent and child to-day. Children, young men and women, behold *He submitted Himself.* If ever a child might have claimed exemption, He might. But no! no! no!! Thus it became Him, for thus it was *right.* And *so,* "The child Jesus grew in wisdom and stature, and in favor with God and man."

III.

THE WORSHIP OF THE MAGI.

"*Now when* Jesus *was born in Bethlehem of* Judæa *in the days of Herod the king, behold, there came wise men from the east to Jerusalem, saying, Where is He that is born King of the Jews? for we have seen His star in the east, and are come to worship Him.* . . . *And when they were come into the house, they saw the young child with Mary His mother, and fell down, and worshipped Him: and when they had opened their treasures, they presented unto Him gifts, gold, and frankincense, and myrrh.*"
—MATTHEW ii. 1, 2, 11.

THE WORSHIP OF THE MAGI.

I FIND it quite impossible to do other than continue the theme of our past two Sabbaths' meditation. The interest you have manifested in the study of the Christ life is to me hopeful and helpful. It makes me feel that He has been reborn in every interested soul; and that He will *unfold* in us as we love Him with our *minds*, and *exfoliate* with beauty as we love Him with our *hearts;* so that again the world shall be glad to see Him come *in us*, to bless, to cheer, and to save.

In studying the circumstances of the early years of Jesus—His mother, His home, His preparation for His life's work—we beheld the constant presence of the overruling Father, directing all that pertained to the development of His Son incarnate in the flesh. The record also gives occasional glimpses of a wide interest beyond the range of our little orb. The heavenly world seemed to be somewhat astir, and the new concern seemed to have centred around this part of the universe. And, indeed, it had seemed at first as if Galilee and Bethlehem were the favored places for the attention of the Heavenly Father and His angels.

But before we go on with the narrative as it relates to Palestine, we have an incident recorded by Matthew which commands our consideration. It is one which impresses us with the important fact that the same Father of all was not only busy preparing blessings for His children at Nazareth and Jerusalem, and guiding the feet of Him that was to bring good tidings to men; but that He was busy in *other* parts of this world of His, guiding *other* feet into the light of this salvation which was "unto all people;" that one class without the other "should not be made perfect." So spake the Father the words afterward enunciated by the Son; who, in turn, spake *always* the words of His Father: "Other sheep have I which are not of this fold, them also will I bring."

In our past discourses we made no reference at all to the revelations which accompanied the birth of Jesus. It pleased God not only to send His Son, but to send words of testimony to man that His gift of love had come. "There were shepherds abiding in the field by night." They had a revelation made to them in simple literal form. It might be called, by some, a direct revelation; and yet, in fact, it was no more direct than others. It was a revelation through the media they could best understand. And so the sky filled with visible angels, and the words fell upon their *ears*, and thus into their hearts. Another revelation came *in the temple* to one Simeon. He had been waiting a long time for the "consolation of Israel." He had seen many a babe brought to the temple at the ceremony of purification, but it was revealed to him that *this one* was the long-looked-for hope of the world. The manner of his revelation was that by which he had been told before that "he should not see *death*" till this sight of *life* should be accorded to him. It was a voice to his *soul*, not sounded upon his ear by an angel, but whispered by a spirit. He knew spiritual voices, he was evidently guided by them. Then comes the third revelation referred to in the text. It was a voice to the seekers who were far away in the East. Their mode of worship was through the stars. Long ages ago they had known of the God of Abraham, and also of the God of Israel. Balaam was a Gentile prophet who knew God and knew Israel.

Since that long ago, Jews had been dwellers among them in captivity, and Jewish history was the marvellous story to other nations and peoples. However despised the Jews might be, there was never lost the *thought*—whether believed or doubted—that they were to give the world a messenger divine. All the forms of worship, outside the pure worship of Judaism, partook of the sun worship and the star worship. Moreover, the wise men referred to in the text were the prophets of the land from whence they had come. They were the honest seekers after the truth. Verily they were upward lookers in more senses than the one. It is not for us to speak lightly of the best wisdom of their time and place; for we must remember that other generations shall arise to smile at our credulities and at our doubts. There is much in the wisdom, and especially in the fidelity of to-day, for which our children can reasonably arise to call us blessed; and to those who know how to seek it, there can be found in every age and place the good seed of the kingdom to come. God knew where to seek it and where to find it, and His manner of reaching the seekers was the most natural, the most simple, the most divine. This is truly *father-like*. Simeon could not have read a message in the stars, nor could the shepherds have read the divinity of the babe in the temple. To each, therefore, of His children He sends His message written in the language most familiar to their hearts. These Eastern ones were looking in the stars for the revelation; and if God would find them, He must address His message to them *there* or it would be lost. And so in and among their pondered constellations there appeared one night a new star with a glory about it of so uncommon cast as to lead them to see in it "*His* star." It was a star they expected, to reveal to them the coming King. They were not able to quote to each other those numerous prophecies that Simeon and Anna, and Mary and Elizabeth would rehearse in their expectation; but one they would surely remember, because it was associated with their own history as well as with the Jewish.

The old Eastern prophet, Balaam, sent for to come and curse the Israelites when they were in conflict with Moab, found that the Lord whom he served would not permit such a curse; but indeed turned His curse into a blessing. In the chapter which we read for our lesson to-day (Numbers xxiv.), you remember the solemn and important prophecy of the seventeenth verse, "I shall see Him, but not now; I shall behold Him, but not nigh; there shall come a *star* out of Jacob, and a sceptre shall arise out of Israel and shall smite the corners of Moab and destroy all the children of Seth," etc. This prophecy was not made *to* the Israelites, but *of* them; and its memory led all the surrounding nations to expect, that some day the King of the Jews would rule the world.

There was everything consistent, then, in the appearance of a star to those who sought their truth through that medium. I am well aware that many questions arise in human minds about an interesting event of this kind. I could make for you a very entertaining hour this morning if I rehearsed to you the legends that have been written about these wise men from the East, and about this star. Almost all the questions have had some offered solution. Chrysostom and Augustine declare that there were twelve of them in number; but most writers seem to favor the idea that there were only three. One old writer goes so far as to give us their names, and their country, and their personal appearance. He describes them as representing the three periods of life, and the three divisions of the globe. *Melchior*, an old man and a descendant of Shem; *Caspar*, a ruddy and beardless youth, and a son of Ham, and *Balthasar*, a man in the vigor of middle life, and of the offspring of Japheth. Those of you who have read the interesting "Ben Hur," by Lew Wallace, will recognize these as the names he employs to denote his three Kings of the Orient.

I cannot, however, spend time in repeating to you the legends of men. I know some of you would prefer to hear them, and my sermon would be considered very entertaining and enjoyable were I to tell you what has been written on purpose *for* entertainment, and for enjoyment. But I am not an entertaining preacher, nor have I ever yet condescended to make a stage of my pulpit, or a drama of my reading desk. There are hundreds of enchanting stories about the early life of Jesus, which I have read, but with no honest profit, except to know their uselessness, and to see, in contrast therewith, the abounding beauty of the Gospel's simplicity.

The legends literalize; the Spirit generalizes. The legends multiply forms, the Spirit maketh bare. The legend and the drama confine the truth, the Spirit emancipates it. The language of the drama is "*this one*," the language of the Spirit is "*whosoever*." The language of the play and the legend is "*in this place*," the language of the Spirit is "*wherever*," or "*everywhere*." And so the literalist who makes literature, says, "Melchior and Caspar and Balthasar," while the Spirit says, "wise *men* from the East." The drama dresses them up as *kings*, and clothes them with the drapery of locality and office, forgetting that if God the Father came to them it would be to them as *men*, not as kings; and it would be as *men* they could come to Jerusalem to worship.

If any ask me who were the wise men? I would answer, that there is no information more valuable than what the Spirit has revealed that they were "*men*," and that they were "*wise*." Both of these qualifications may be yours, and can give you personal interest in them.

The question is also asked: Was it a star, or only an appearance of such? Astronomy has quite rightly given its research into this question, and interesting facts are brought to light which bear upon the narrative. But there are many legends about the star, and many curious inquiries about its guidance. There is a very interesting book, entitled, "The Star of our Lord," which, I think, repays the reader for his time, and brings some very striking truths to light. But there are many other books, and many other ideas and opinions, that might just as easily be true as this one. My own belief forms into a devotion that there was a star; astronomical search does not give any cause for doubt. It is reasonable, with all the scientific investigation, to believe that there did appear for the first time to earth on that occasion a new star. It takes a long time for a star, when first lighted, to send its rays to so great a distance as this; and there is much analogy moving all along between the natural and the spiritual. So, as it was, "when the fulness of time was come," that God sent His Son, it is not at all incongruous to believe that He who said, "I will make a new heavens and a new earth" should show signs in heaven above as well as in the earth beneath. But doubters want to literalize here again, and ask, "How could a star move along so low down in our atmosphere as to show them just what house to stop at?" I have scarcely patience to deal with small questions. We must know that when a man says, "I see a star," he sees it only in, and through a few of its rays that touch his eye. It were not at all a necessity that the Heavenly Father should have to disarrange the whole system—as stupid doubters would argue—in order to light them to their destined spot. But what if He did? Was not the cause a worthy one? Had not these very truth seekers been always giving too much worship to the stars and all the mighty host of the firmament, and too little to Him who holdeth the stars in His right hand, and calls them by their names? Would it not be a beautiful father's lesson to themselves on that auspicious day or night, not only to show His fatherhood in the incarnate Son, but to teach them hereafter to say, "He ordereth the worlds in their courses, He knoweth the stars also?"

But have not the stars always been guides to human travellers? Has not the Dipper pointed the unlettered bondman to the north in every day and place? Was not Abraham *star*-led, when he journeyed from Chaldea to Egypt, across the naked plains of the desert; and now, while I speak to you, are not the sons of sail, trusted with priceless lives, and freighted with the wealth of nations, crossing the oceans and the seas, *star*-led from continent to continent? Why, ever since upward-gazing man has been upon the earth, it has been the office of the stars to guide; and this guiding star which led the seekers unto Bethlehem, so far from being incongruous or unnatural, only raised the natural a little higher for the lofty occasion in honor of the coming of the Lord of Nature. And ever since that guiding star led the distant Orientals to find the western house where the child dwelt with His mother, has there been to every seeking soul a new star in his firmament which leads him on, not to the house in Bethlehem, which has crumbled long ago to the dust of earth, but to the "house of God not made with hands, eternal in the heavens?"

"Wise men!" From the schools of the best thought and most wide-reaching study came these men to see and worship. The Christ has always been subject to the scrutiny of the loftiest intellects and has always had the "wisest" men worshipping at His feet. The greatest metaphysicians—Sir William Hamilton and Jonathan Edwards—worshipped at the feet of Jesus. The greatest of astronomers—Herschel, Faraday, Newton—worshipped at the feet of Jesus. The greatest poets—Milton, Dante, Longfellow, Whittier, and a thousand more—worshippers at the feet of Jesus. The wisest writer on law—Blackstone—a worshipper of Jesus. The mightiest intellect of America's last century—Franklin; the mightiest intellect of England's present prowess —Gladstone—worshippers at the feet of Jesus.

Going back again to our text we read that the distinct purpose with which these Oriental students started from their distant home was to come and worship the King of the Jews, which, without doubt, they recognized as a king with wider realm than that of Jewry, and with loftier throne than that of earthly sway. The Jews had never been a people like other peoples. The surrounding nations had always known them with reference to their divine relation. They always professed themselves the people of the Most High. If surrounding nations fell before them in battle, it was believed that their God had given them the victory. If the heathen gained a victory over Israel, it was believed that the sin of the Jews had alienated their God from them. And so it is the easiest possible thought for us that these wise men came to welcome a divine prince, come to rule over and bless all nations. It will be interesting for us now to go with them to the place of worship, and mark the character of their obeisance.

It is written, "they fell down and worshipped Him; and when they had opened their treasures, they presented unto Him gifts; gold, and frankincense, and myrrh." I do not know whether they were disappointed at finding the object of their search to be only an unconscious infant. Certainly there is no record of surprise or of regret. And if there was either, or both, they were soon overcome, and were not permitted to stand in the way of their adoration. It would not be unnatural to suppose that they expected to see a king, and receive some recognition in turn for their compliment and gift. Indeed, we can hardly imagine other than that they expected, when they started out, to bring back some blessing from the mouth of the new monarch, which they would deliver with pride to their fellows who waited their return. There is nothing in the narrative to **warrant** this supposition; but I read it out of the book of human nature as we all find it. And I have not supposed it to the detriment of the honesty and integrity of the devotees before us. And be it said to their honor, that they withheld nothing they had brought for a king, when they were introduced into the presence of a child.

But, perhaps, we have done them injustice in supposing as we have done. Let us then believe that they came to worship without any expectation of reward or return of honor upon themselves. For verily that is the true worship. Worship is not receiving, it is **giving**. And one reason why our worship is often outstripped in

THE WORSHIP OF THE MAGI. 61

its devotion and ardor of sacrifice by the idolater is, they are not accustomed to look for any immediate recognition from their god. They go over and over again and offer their gift in the dark; and they thus satisfy their own sense of duty or of devotion. If these Magi had been accustomed to the shrine of Baal or of Ashtaroth, though wise enough to look beyond, and long for some being—the author of both themselves and their objects or worship—they were not accustomed to receive any gifts or words of comfort or of hope. And so it is possible that their worship at this time was pure from all expectation of reward, a real outflow of delight, joy, yea love, that the great veil of nature had been rent and the Father was coming to speak with men. And gifts were the tokens of their worship. Gifts are always the language of the heart. God has not left one child too poor on earth to express its love. The beggar boy will give his crust to his little sweetheart and go hungry himself, feeling that pain in love is sweet. There has never been a time or place where this rule was abrogated. It cannot be abrogated. It is a law of our being. "Where the treasure is there will the heart be also," is quite as true in the inverse order, where the heart is there will the treasure be also.

"And they presented unto Him gifts; gold, and frankincense, and myrrh." These were their most valuable possessions, and so represented the highest form of inward estimation. Many have found a peculiar significance in the triple form of gift, but the peculiar is too small for the world to contemplate. They gave the best they had; that is the valuable idea in it. And it is the whole secret of true worship. Do you say, "God is a spirit, and they that worship Him must worship Him in spirit and in truth?" Verily! verily! And was not that just what these men did? Did they say: "This child can know no value in our gifts, and so there can be no worship; we can keep them to ourselves for all the good they can do Him, or all the appreciation He can form of them." No; such thoughts as those are left for our poor, narrow thinkers of to-day. They worshipped in the spirit, their hearts poured out their gifts; and somehow, somewhere, they believed the love they struggled to express was known to that unseen One who gave the mind its reason, and the heart its love, and the hand its material gifts to bestow. We, who have no gifts, are the ones that do not worship in spirit and in truth. They who have no spirit need little form in which to express themselves. The big hearts need more than words to make their ardor and devotion known. "Sounding brass and tinkling cymbal" are the expression of a loveless, heartless, spiritless **worship**.

THE WORSHIP OF THE MAGI. 63

Now, you all know I am speaking the truth in this matter. You know that the one at whose feet you would lay your gold, or frankincense, or myrrh, or whatever you count your treasures, is the one you love and worship. Take me and show me where you put your treasures, and I will show you your temple and your god.

There is no way so true of measuring a man's devotion to any object or cause as to ascertain what is his money-devotion to it.

You are all satisfied that the wise men told a true story when they said, "We have seen His star in the East, and have come to worship Him." You are satisfied that their worship is real, when you read that they "opened up their treasures"—treasures to them, mind you—and impoverished themselves for His sake. This is the evidence they left behind that their visit was a success.

Now, there is one more question which seems to arise over this incident. It is, What was the value of this visit? Who were benefited by it, and how were they benefited? We must be brief in just noting the answers to these questions.

First, then, *the child Jesus* was benefited. The gifts did really reach Him, and touch His life and add to His comfort, in a world where He came in poverty. Sorrow had already begun to lower like distant thunder, in the voice of the cruel Herod. A long journey for the young child and His mother and Joseph must be made into Egypt. And from somewhere gold must come to accomplish the journey, and construct the history of the Messiah. The gold of the wise men went directly into the history of the kingdom, and into the very experience of the Christ. It verily had to do with the maintenance of His life. It is useless to ask, had not their gold been forthcoming, would not other means have been secured? No doubt they would. Other gold would have done the work— not theirs. But their gold did it; and this was to them high honor, whenever the story should reach them. It is the same with our gifts to-day. We may sometimes say: "If I withhold, the cause will not suffer." That may or may not be so. But *we* will suffer. We will lose our contribution to the history of the kingdom, when we verily withhold our portion of ministration to the comfort of the young child. The Gospel is like a young child yet in many localities. Worldly forces seek to put away its life; and the gifts of its devotees maintain its propagation and life in the community where it has come to abide and bless.

But, secondly, by the gifts and visit of the Magi, the *cause* of the Christ was benefited. It stirred up the whole community of Priests and Levites and Scribes to search the records and begin to "seek the Lord, if haply they might feel after Him and find Him"—formally, at least—in their records and Scriptures. It brought such a revival of interest as had not been known for years within a dead Church. And so it is to-day. Let a few outsiders, called by the Church sinners, Gentiles, heathens, come into the Church's quarters and begin to worship—laying down their gifts at the feet of the Church, and worshipping the name professedly revered there—and it wakes up the preacher, and elders, and deacons, and stewards, and leaders, and a revival is sure to follow. And,

Thirdly, the *wise men* themselves were benefited. It is perhaps not possible for us to know how joyfully they returned to their own land. They came to Bethlehem guided by a star. They left for home, and the Lord God led them by a way they knew not. It is significantly recorded they "departed into their own country another way," being warned of God in a dream. They needed no star now between them and God. They would no longer worship stars, but see in them only the media of God's lighting His children's way. But they must find the blessing that is promised to the followers of the Son of God. They must learn that in the heaven where the new King reigns supreme, "there shall be no night there," and they need neither candle, nor star, nor light of the sun, "for the Lord God and the Lamb are the light thereof."

Did Philip go unto Nathanael and say, " We have found Him of whom Moses in the law and the prophets did write—Jesus of Nazareth, the Son of Joseph?" Did the woman of Samaria go into her own city with the tidings, " Come see a man that told me all things that ever I did; is not this the Christ?" So may we verily believe that the wise men returned to the East and said unto their own, in the language of the old prophet Balaam, fulfilled, " We have seen Him, and that now, and have beheld Him, and that nigh. There hath come a star out of Jacob and a sceptre hath arisen in Israel; out of Jacob hath He come that shall have dominion." And thus shall the seed of the kingdom have found its way to those distant souls that sought a way of peace and a heart to love and adore, who should in turn find their way to Jerusalem, and join that promiscuous throng in saying, " How hear we every man in our own tongue in which we were born: Parthians and Medes and Elamites, and the dwellers in Mesopotamia and Cappadocia, and Pontus and Asia, Phrygia and Pamphylia, Cretes and Arabians, we do hear them speak in our own tongues the wonderful works of God."

IV.
THE CHRIST PROCLAIMED.

"*And Jesus answering said unto him, Suffer it to be so now: for thus it becometh us to fulfil all righteousness. . . . And Jesus, when He was baptized, went up straightway out of the water; and, lo, the heavens were opened unto Him, and he saw the Spirit of God descending like a dove, and lighting upon Him. And lo a voice from heaven, saying, This is my beloved Son, in whom I am well pleased.*"

MATTHEW iii. 15-17.

THE CHRIST PROCLAIMED.

TWO weeks ago, we gave our morning hour to the study of the early life of the boy Jesus; and we made some reference to the years of silence which followed upon His return to Galilee from Jerusalem, at twelve years of age. The few expressive words of revelation teach us that all truths which He should know, and afterwards proclaim, must pass through His own experience.

Simply it is announced: "He grew in stature." And so do we see, that He passed through that common experience when boys wish they could be men, but find it impossible to become so, except by the law of growth. He was speaking, then, from simply human experience when, in after days, He said, "Which of you, by taking thought, can add unto His stature one cubit?"

And it is written, "He grew in wisdom." His mind was instructed as were other minds, by reading and by observation. "Have ye not read?" was a common expression of His, after He came into His public ministrations; and this would signify that He was in possession of His knowledge of Jewish, and other history, by the same means as the ordinary students of His day. And He was keenly observant. He loved truth. Living in Galilee, not very far from the sea, He became acquainted with the various occupations of men. He watched the fishers draw their nets, and divide their fish—putting the good into vessels, and casting the bad away. He saw the merchantman seeking goodly pearls. He walked the fields, and watched the sower go forth to sow; and He went back over the same ground to see how came up that seed which He had watched the sower cast. He saw the rocky spots, and the thorns, and the trodden wayside, where the seeds did not mature. He saw the tares grow up among the wheat, and marked men gather them and cast them into the fire to be burned. He watched His mother make the loaves they ate within the home. Their family just required three measures of meal, and He watched His mother put in the little leaven, and marked its peculiar spreading power as it leavened the whole lump. And so on, all through the course of His life, He gathered information; and stored His mind with matters which seemed to be of interest to humanity. By all these transactions of men and women, He learned the thoughts of human hearts, and marked the ideals that moved them on from day to day. Everything was of importance to Him, as a revelation of what was in man. And thus, man became an increasingly interesting subject of thought to Him, every added year of His growing life.

But there is one other important word written concerning His early life : " He waxed strong in Spirit." This has reference to a feature of His development different from either of the others. Stature, wisdom, Spirit. These three mark the fact that His nature— that which He took upon Him—was the simple human nature which God gave to man when He made him in His own image, and which now He would restore to that image before the gaze of men. The simple record of these three constituents undergoing the law of growth, is always to me one of the refutations of that form of thought which some hold of the conditional immortality of our nature ; making it, in creation, a soulless animalism. But this thought has no special reference to our theme of to-day.

When we read, however, of how He " waxed strong in Spirit," we come to the secret spring of His life. All other exercises of human function find their final value here. The Spirit is the true author and finisher of every action of body or mind. It would matter but little how He had developed His mental resources, or how He brought His body to perfection through careful discipline, if these had not been so prepared, to minister to a Spirit worthy of their service. We can readily conceive Him studying the why of human actions on every side of Him. From the day of His sitting in the temple asking the questions of the doctors, we may believe He asked many questions of the sons of men. And as the outcome of these studies and inquiries, He would find what kind of a spirit possessed mankind. And He would also find that within Himself there was a different valuation placed upon things, from what man usually placed upon them. He would find some relics of high and noble purpose; some strugglings here and there after a better form of life; but, in the main, He would come to feel that man was really lost to the gracious purpose of his being, as man. He was led more and more each passing day to realize that man did not understand his own nature nor his Father's will concerning him. And He was conscious all the while that His own soul found, in fellowship with God, and with the creatures of God, and with the works of God, and with God in the history of His people, an experience, a comfort, a life, almost entirely unknown to His human brethren about Him. As He read over the dealings of God with men in the past, it seemed to Him clear enough that God sought the hearts of men, and sought to establish a kingdom of love and brotherhood in the earth. But it seemed to His fellows as if God had always been a divider and a respecter of persons. He began to feel the indwelling divine taking hold of His enlarging human spirit; for it must be known that only as the human put on its maturities, could the divine show its fulness in Him. And so it came to pass that as He grew, He found Himself more and more closely related to every man by the interest his very nature took in them; and, at the same time, He found Himself more and more different—in the law of the Spirit which ruled Him—from those He was fast learning to love, even in their errors and sins.

Two things grew upon Him with intensity, the greatness and the ruin of man. These, of course, set up the problem in His heart, Can man be redeemed? And such a question to such a soul would never be put aside till answered. To Him, now, redemption would begin to mean spiritual regeneration and restoration. If a Messiah is the need of the world, it must be one that will rule over hearts, and rule unto harmony and brotherly love. From what He could see of the kings of the earth, they only exercised authority, to keep their fellows under their sway. And that seemed to bring no fruit of good to man. The great world of men was divided and subdivided, so that each sought its own party life, even to the death of all others. The whole spirit of things was wrong. He could see it, even as a man.

The Church, *it* was as one of the parties. It was not for the people; rather, the people were for it. He had seen the "Corbans" robbing the aged of the peace and comfort which the divine law of Moses had ordained for them; and the exactions of the priesthood binding heavy burdens, grievous, indeed, to be borne. All this only revealed to Him that the spirit of kings, and the spirit of priests, and the spirit of teachers was all astray from the right. It could not win hearts. It showed no love for the creatures with whom it was in exercise. It sought to be "ministered unto." It made slaves of men. And this would naturally wake up, in His own spirit, that sympathy and sorrow for the oppressed and unblessed which He afterwards displayed everywhere; and also that holy anger toward those whose true office should be guides, and leaders, and helpers of the people, but who were actually the greatest factors in their degradation. Under all these influences, we say, " He waxed strong in Spirit." Stronger and stronger His spirit would swell under the increasing evidences before Him of human need and absence of remedy. "He looked, and there was none to pity." And He found no one able to commune with Him in Spirit over the case. His mother could, to some extent, encourage Him that His feelings were right, but could offer no solution of the awful problem.

Can we not,—God forgive us, for we hardly can, our hearts are so narrow and cold,—Can we not a little realize how such a spirit would desire to go right out and seek an alleviation of the sufferings of the world? But, think of it! Go where, how, to whom? Where begin the awful work? No one will understand His mission, or be ready to lend a helping hand. The kings will not lend their power to Him. The priests will question His authority; and being of another spirit, will not warm to His mission. Verily would they say, "When Messias cometh He will tell us all things and put all things to rights."

And so I think we can well imagine the restlessness of love, and zeal, and desire, and will, that waxed in the spirit of the man Jesus as He grew up toward thirty years of age. And we may here say that it was becoming more and more possible for Him as a man to feel the presence of the Deity within Himself. He felt that He had the witness of the Spirit of His Father testifying to His own spirit, waxing daily in warmth of ardor for the children of men.

In our bewilderment of thought about a dual nature in the Christ, we wonder if at all times He did not know and feel the fulness of His Deity and the purpose and work of His life. But we must remember that if Deity was present always to *know*, then as God He must know that He was not yet a man—not yet a knowing, conscious, mature man; and so the coalescing was not yet complete. And so as man, the human could only, by and through human means of understanding, come to know its fellowship and oneness with the divine. And so the time was fast approaching when this maturity of consciousness should come. While Jesus of Nazareth could scarcely work at His daily avocation for the fiery flame of loving passion within, He heard of John the Baptist preaching in the wilderness of Judæa, and saying, "Repent ye, for the kingdom of heaven is at hand." He heard that John's message was one of honest, practical worth; that all ranks and classes of society were affected by it. Priests, Scribes, Pharisees, soldiers, publicans and peasants, wealth, rank and poverty, heard stern words of rebuke for sin, and a proclamation that the kingdom of righteousness was to be set up. This would be a call to Him. If the cause of man is now to be undertaken, He is born to an important part in it.

"Then," oh, the important step!—"then cometh Jesus to Jordan." I see Him set out upon the journey. He leaves the home in Nazareth, and the shop, and his mother, and sisters, and brethren. They have learned long ago not to question too closely His thoughts and purposes, for He is too deep for them to fathom. He realizes that He is to go into an awful conflict with all earth and hell and sin. Impelled by all within, and called by the outward news of John's announcement, He sets out from Galilee to Jordan, over a road He had often travelled to see the passover lamb slain, and attend the feasts of commemoration. He " was alone, and of the people there was none with Him;" none in person, none in spirit. But He communed with His Father, and was led of His will and of His Spirit; and His own spirit solemnly submitted, even though He saw the cross, and the rejection and the failure apparent. But He felt that though He should fail to convince in life alone, the world should learn that there is a love unto death, and that this is the love of God for men. Nobody else was revealing it. The world was dying for it. All were seeking their own, and so came the sins which John was thundering against in the wilderness of Judæa. With solemn majesty, I think, He moved through the excited crowd that surrounded the Baptist at the river, and the fierce denunciations ceased at His approach ; and the strong, brave face of the greatest prophet fell into the expression of a child, as the man Jesus, impelled by the Deity within—nay, not impelled, for there was a sweet and perfect harmony of spirit—went forward and submitted Himself for baptism by the prophet of the Lord God.

And so we see that this Jordan scene of Jesus being baptized was the end of the beginning, and the beginning of the end. It was the point to which the eighteen silent years legitimately culminated. It was the point from which the three most eventful of all human years took their legitimate beginning.

The appearance upon the scene of our narrative of John the Baptist awakes our interest in him. He was a chosen servant of God to do a special work. Short, brief, concise was to be his work; but it required a brave courageous spirit to do it. He was obliged to assume an independent line of life, to gain strength over the conventionalities of his day. He was independent in his food, clothing and dwelling. And these were large factors in human life, in that day as well as this. The study of the Baptist's character and work may be worthy some time of a special study; but at present he is only used to introduce the silent Christ to publicity and place. He was great as a prophet—but the "least in the kingdom was greater than he." He was only the vestibule to Christianity's temple. He preached the coming of the Christ. Jesus was the gospel which all others preach. John erred and doubted. Christ never made a mistake or a retraction. John died a victim simply of a woman's lust. Jesus died a priest; none could take away His life. John's death did nothing for the race; Christ's death saved the race. There was no story of John's resurrection; they set no seal or watch. When the disciples laid his headless body away in the tomb, they went away and disorganized, never to come together again. Christ rose from the grave, gathered His disciples, established His Church, and went home to heaven to bestow gifts upon them to the fulness of all things. We will return, then, to the hero of our study.

We had just seen Jesus of Nazareth coming into the presence of the Baptist. A stranger to the multitude, He stood there, a sweet, mysterious looking face, which so impressed the prophet that he spake of Him as he had spoken of no other. John was a keen observer, or he would never have been able to read the hearts of those who came near unto him. If he could so discern one company as to say, "O generation of vipers, who hath warned you to flee the wrath to come," he could read the transparency of innocence in the face of his friend Jesus. "I have need to be baptized of Thee, and comest Thou to me?" John would have said that quickly had he seen and known Jesus every day of the past years. What is the real meaning of those words of John recorded by the evangelist—" I knew Him not" —we may differently opine. Doubtless "he knew Him not" as the Messiah. He did not go out knowingly to proclaim on behalf of his cousin Jesus of Nazareth. But when Jesus came to him and said, "Suffer it to be so," and the baptism was performed in solemn silence, the scene was one where heaven and earth flashed sparks of touch; and mercy and truth met together; and righteousness and peace kissed each other; and the nuptials of a marriage were solemnized, and God the Father pronounced the benediction.

"And Jesus went up straightway out of the water, and, lo, the heavens opened, and he saw the Spirit of God descending like a dove, and lighting upon Him; and lo a voice from heaven, saying, This is My beloved Son, in whom I am well pleased." Oh! it is God and man, heaven and earth, the same story from the beginning. That dove unites the records, and gives the same signature to all. At the first creation, in the beginning of the Old Testament, we find it recorded that the Spirit of God "brooded over the face of the waters," like a dove, with outstretched wings, preparing the world to be the abode of life. And at the second creation, the dove's wings hovered over the waters of the deluge, announcing the end of the judgment of death, and the ministration of the new unfolding of life. And at the new creation, when the world is to be born again, the Holy Spirit comes in the form of a dove, and broods over the waters of this baptism, symbol of the new covenant of peace, and the abolition of death, and bringing of life and immortality to light through the Gospel.

But why was Jesus baptized? John had said, "I indeed baptize with water unto repentance." Surely it was not "unto repentance" He was baptized! Well, no; and yet, yes. He was not a sinner that had need to repent of His sins; but, if He was, He would repent. He believed in repentance; it was of God, it was of life, it was such as He was quite willing to subscribe to. And then, there was something in His experience in common with the repentance of us all. There was a putting away of the world. He was renouncing the world—home, mother, means of livelihood, friends, all. These would be washed away symbolically by the running stream. It was to Him in that sense, not an absolution, but an ablution, a washing of Spirit from any and everything that had, to any extent, divided His interest. This was His complete consecration to the work of His Father; and, therefore, it really deserved the divine recognition. Then and there He entered into the kingdom, "Into which the forerunner, even Jesus, having entered," He could invite all others to follow.

"Thus it becometh us to fulfil all righteousness." Oh! what lessons for us to learn. How common for us to ask relief from any rules and regulations! If any one could have passed into the kingdom without this formal baptism, it was He. He did not disclaim the homage that John paid to Him—He never did disclaim honor, however great; but He said, "Let it be so," for it is becoming in us to fulfil, to exalt, to honor all righteousness. Had He refused, or passed by the baptism, how could He bid all others be baptized? His refusal would have been not a constructive force, but a breach in the line. He wanted to touch humanity everywhere. He connected Himself, therefore, by this act with the whole of the Old Testament history, through John; and He connected the Old, through John, to Himself and the New. There was a propriety in all that He said and did; and He believed in propriety. He wanted to submit Himself; He had learned submission all His life at Nazareth. Entering as He was upon a new sphere of action, He was still submissive for the sake of fitness. Such a submission was no acknowledgment on His part of sin in Himself, any more than the taking of the oath of allegiance on entering upon an official post would imply any past heart disloyalty on the part of a British subject to his sovereign.

And now, my dear listeners, what is our lessson as the followers of Christ from this study? Is it not that those of us who are interested in the world's salvation, and have "grown in wisdom and waxed strong in Spirit," should begin to feel at some time a culmination to all this growing interest, which leads us up to a threshold of full consecration? The baptism of Jesus turned out to be a baptism of the Holy Ghost. He had His "pentecost" at Jordan. We must not think of our water baptism as any correlate of His baptism. We have been instructed by His life, we have been taught at His feet; we have been His followers for years, and have surely come to desire the redemption of our fellow-men. Though we may realize all this; do we not feel that there is a baptism that should wash from us all our worldly interest and leave us pure to pursue the work of laying down our lives for the brethren? Our lives! I mean the lives we have wrought up in stature, and wisdom, and spirit. Is there no prompting this morning that comes from the spirit within, to enter into the glorious work of the kingdom? Is there no voice from without, where we hear the sound of the prophet's voice calling aloud to the sinners to "Repent, for the kingdom of heaven is at hand?" Is it not meet, becoming, that we should come to the same Jordan where sinners are turning from sin to seek the kingdom of Jesus; and put ourselves under the same influences to be the forerunners of others into the kingdom. Why should we refuse to submit ourselves on the ground that we are now holy, and need no baptism? Let us humble ourselves to the level of the lowest, that the blessed Spirit may descend upon us and approve our consecration to the work of leading the souls of our fallen brothers and sisters into the gate of the kingdom.

I believe that the path of duty lies thus before us now; untrodden, and beautifully pure. If we be anything of true men, we cannot look forward unmoved. An enthusiasm will verily come upon us. A sense of the presence of one higher and greater than ourselves we cannot help but feel, choosing us for this work and sending us forth to do it. If we yield to it we shall be lifted above our former selves into a region of higher usefulness and higher delight, where thought is supplanted by inspiration. We shall grasp with our very greatest strength the new world of our aspiration. We shall not wish, but we shall *will*, to be pure, true, faithful. We shall consecrate ourselves to the holy duty.

And this will be a partial exhibition in us of the meaning of Christ's baptism. So shall we come to know something of the thoughts and feelings which filled His spirit when in the waters of the Jordan, whose ripples formed about His feet,—He began in self-devotion, sad and resolute, and calm, His gracious ministry of love. Oh, my dear brothers of humanity, in such a service, if you want an impulse, you will verily find it; an impulse which, though you falter at times in the strife, will never leave or forsake you. When we return to these studies we will mark how well that work the Master here undertook was carried on. He had opposition, fierce and unfair; but there was never one failure. He met obstacles more and mightier than we can ever meet; but ever nobler and firmer, wiser, and tenderer, and stronger, rose the Spirit of Jesus of Nazareth—now the Christ—to accomplish the Father's will, till in the last triumphant hour He could majestically cry, "I have finished the work Thou didst give Me to do." "Father, into Thy hands I commend My spirit."

YESTERDAY, TO-DAY AND TO-MORROW

MUSIC IN "SONGS OF CALVARY."

Yesterday I wander'd in the paths of sin,
   Danger all around me, death straight before me ;
Yesterday the world crazed my soul with its din—
   Mercy sang her sweet notes in vain.

CHORUS.

  Oh ! hear her calling, over and over,
    Oh ! hear her calling, listen ! be still !
  I cannot bear to resist any longer,
    Speak once again and I'll hearken,—I will.

To-day I'm standing asking, Oh, what shall I do ?
   Sorrow overwhelms me, Calvary constrains me ;
To-day I'm halting here with forgiveness in view,
   Mercy sings her sweet notes again.

To morrow I am dreading, for my foes will assail,
   Evil passions in me, tempters all about me ;
To-morrow I am sure all my own strength will fail,
   Mercy thou shalt not sing in vain.

V.

THE BEGINNING OF THE WORK.

(THE WILDERNESS AND THE DEVIL.)

" Then was Jesus led up of the spirit into the the wilderness to be tempted of the devil. And when He had fasted forty days and forty nights, He was afterward an hungred. . . . And . . . the tempter came to Him." . .

MATTHEW iv. 1-4.

THE BEGINNING OF THE WORK.

(THE WILDERNESS AND THE DEVIL.)

WE resume this morning, after a month's absence, our interesting studies of the great life—of *the* life—of *life*. And we are most anxious students, I know; for we believe that in the understanding of the life of Jesus Christ we shall find the secret of our own lives as followers of Him. Without the knowledge and the following of Him, we believe the secret must ever remain hidden, and even the light that is in us be darkness.

In our last study, we left Him in an honored place "becoming all righteousness," and so called the "beloved Son of God." He had just graduated, as it were, in His life studies, and the "commencement exercises" had been conducted at His baptism in the Jordan river. His life work was now before Him. Living men are not consecrated for rest. When we bring our all to the altar, it is as a "living sacrifice" for a "service;"

acknowledged as "reasonable." When the baptism of the Holy Ghost came upon Him and registered His name a "Son," "*then*," it is recorded, was He "led up of that Spirit into the wilderness."

It is important for us to bear in mind that the record before us is history. It has told us for what end He was led into the wilderness. And so, with the record before us, we march forward with the curtain of His future always uplifted by our information. But we must, for the time, strive to dispossess ourselves of these facts. We read too fast. Already we know that He was led into the wilderness to be tempted of the devil. And we know how he was tempted and how it all came out. But just suppose ourselves on the Jordan bank again with Him, *not knowing* the next step in the journey. See Him now separated from all the life of former years, without plan, without friend, without home, with only one all absorbing purpose pushing Him on, and that *one* to be the means of conveying the Father's saving love to the race. How is it to be conveyed? He wants it to be seen, to be seen well, to be seen by all, to be seen in its fulness. And it is to be seen *in man*. If He be God, He must be God contracted to a span. If He be the Son of God, He must be the Son of God as man. He must move forward, then, as man. And so He must look up at all times and say, " Father, into Thy hands I commend My spirit."

"He is led up into the wilderness." For what? That remains to be seen. He must begin His work there. He must commence at the lowest point. It was into the wilderness the first Adam was driven when he was cast out of the garden for his disobedience. When He, the second Adam, comes up as a victor, He must come up out of the wilderness. The wilderness is the physical expression of sin's work. Sin makes gardens into wildernesses Wild men, wild beasts, wild fruits, wild flowers, are the habitants of the wilderness. Lawless, untamed, ungovernable, are the characteristics of dwellers there. He had never tasted the wilderness experience. He had seen life under favorable circumstances : a good mother, a comfortable home, a beautiful locality, kind friendships, religious oversight, food convenient, clothing all that was needful. For the work He had undertaken, He had now renounced all these. Here begins the awful abstinence. No roof to shelter His head, as at Nazareth ! No mother to speak even a word of encouragement, as did Mary ! No food when the time for morning and evening meal should return, as in the old home ! No brother, or sister, or friend; no Priest, or Levite, or holy voice, to speak a promise or rehearse a precept. The wilderness and the devil !

The devil would make the whole earth a wilderness.

THE BEGINNING OF THE WORK.

Every better part now seen by mortal eye is the partial victory of the seeds of truth sown "at sundry times, and in divers manners, by the prophets." But now the Son has come to see, and to feel, the wilderness. The "wild beasts," Mark says, were there. And He must be touched with the feeling even of their curse. He must live among them; they uncaring for Him, and avoiding Him; when as man, they should court Him, love Him, serve Him, worship Him. "He came," in the wilderness, "to His own" beasts, "and they received Him not." He had not a being to lay His hand upon and caress. These are some phases of His privations.

"Forty days and forty nights." This means the *full time*. It stands to represent the utmost limit of physical endurance without food and shelter. It was not for a few days He was tried. It was not a taste of the bitter that He took. He went to the extreme point, to the very threshold of starvation, to where hunger gave its keenest, sharpest bite. It is the last craving! Home, friends, shelter, one by one are forgotten in the overwhelming cry of the exhausting frame. Does He ask, I wonder, What meaneth all this? Time only can give to the human the answer in full. But there is answer enough to satisfy for the present. It is part of the cup He took in hand.

It is part of the earth's curse, part of the degradation of man, part of the sorrows the human has been called by its sins to endure. And He had made no reserve in His consecration. He has utterly renounced any claim on anything, even on life itself, that He might do "the will of Him that sent Him." The end was worthy the means. And, moreover, the Being to whom He had committed all His care was worthy the confidence reposed in Him. Indeed, He was the Father. The Son need not be anxious for the "where to lay His head," or the wherewithal to feed His mouth; because He knew His Father held the infinite bountifulness of all earthly environment. His accepted dependence was like that of the "fowls of the air," and the "lilies of the field," which are fed and clothed by the unseen arm above and underneath the earth. His poverty was really the boundless affluence which always feeds the humble and the poor in Spirit.

When He comes to speak the beatitudes on the mountain-side, He will speak them all from experience. He will have proven that "Blessed are the poor in spirit, for theirs is the kingdom of heaven," and "Blessed are the meek, for they shall inherit the earth;" and "Blessed are they that hunger and thirst after righteousness, or for righteousness' sake, for they shall be filled." So was it, therefore, that He was "led by the Spirit into the wilderness," to fast, to abstain, to be deprived, for the full season, and to the full extent, of "forty days and forty nights."

A serious and important lesson there must be in all this for His followers; for His Church who are now to do His work in the world, and especially, I would say, for His apostles and ministers, who are to lead that Church in its mighty and all-glorious work. It is to me, my brethren, as though He was saying now, "Before you enter upon your great office, come apart with Me into the wilderness; see how the tempter sought to mislead Me as I was entering upon Mine. As he tempted Me, so will he tempt you. See how in answering him I have taught you the true nature of My kingdom, and the true laws of My mission. Study these, that you, too, may have wherewith to answer the tempter in your time of trial." Let us mark how very applicable such a study is to us to-day; it will help us to take interest in it. I do confidently believe that the Church of God in the world, led by ardent souls, both ministerial and lay, are very eager to prosecute this highest work with all the speed and all the zeal they can muster. They long for the coming of the kingdom of righteousness and joy. They are impatient in the desire to gain a speedy triumph for that kingdom. They see the awful need of salvation for the sons of men. Their hearts are moved, as never before, with a sense of the errors that fill men's minds, and the evils that afflict men's hearts. They have confidence, stronger than in all the past, that God the Father has provided a ransom and a relief for all the sins of His wandering children. They have undertaken the task. They claim to speak for God, the blessed words to His lost ones. They stand forth to witness in their lives that these are the words of life. They testify to the indwelling Spirit given to man whereby both regeneration and reformation come. Think how much this is like the blessed Jesus, as He set out to begin the work in which His followers were to take afterwards so large a part. There was never set before Him a temptation to abandon the work. Never! That would have been futile, indeed. Let us mark in our studies how the temptation in all its forms, is to gain this great work, this great *right*, by the aid of a little *wrong*; how it is to do God's work zealously, earnestly, lovingly, but not exactly in God's way; how it is to give ourselves to Him, as we believe, for this work; but to give ourselves in our own way; to serve Him, but to choose, to some extent at least, the manner of the service. You don't know how very solemn the whole study of this subject has become to me. It is not the first time I have studied it. It is not the first time I have preached upon it—even to you. But coming to it in the order of approach in which we reach it to-day, it seems as if we enter it by the door, and see it in its truest and most impressive aspects.

At the end of the forty days and forty nights it is recorded that "the tempter came to Him." This is a significant utterance. What had been the conflict of the past days and nights? Had not the tempter come to Him before? Are there long and sore temptations that are not ascribed to the devil? Is there a real, personal devil? I know a writer who says: "Who, or what is the devil of the Christian conception? The devil is the carnal propensity in man, the devil is the arrogance and exaltation of self, the devil is the fondness for wealth and dominion. All that tempts the spiritual man to act in opposition to the laws of the Spirit is the devil." In other words, part of the human nature is the devil. With this I am not in accord. I do believe that when the Spirit plans hard tasks, the flesh may cry for ease, and so a conflict may ensue within. I believe that when wrong ideas have been espoused, and wrong habits contracted thereupon, that an effort at reform under the new light meets the opposition of the old formations. And in all this there is trial, struggle and temptation within. I have no thought that Jesus Christ had formed any evil habits to overcome. So I do not think that any conflict of that particular nature had a place in His experience. But was there not a conflict in those forty days going on in self and of self? He had formed lawful habits; habits of eating and drinking, habits of society and home life, habits of friendly intercourse, habits of gathering and getting, habits of religious association, pleasant and sweet. And now, His being "ministered unto" must cease; His gathering into self and for self, however lawfully, must give place. He must empty Himself. He must be *un*fed, *un*clothed, *un*sheltered, *un*taught, *un*blessed, *un*comforted. Sin must have its destructive work wrought upon His life. He must be "made sin for us who knew no sin," that we might be made righteous through Him. And so I think He trod that wine-press alone. He fought with self as self, and He fought till He conquered. Then came the devil. Yes, a tempter from the realms of sin. A tempter known by reputation to all students of history at least; and a tempter everywhere, where God has spoken to man of a larger universe than this earth, recognized as an agent mighty and powerful. A spirit whose work has traced a dark record upon the hearts of man; and a spirit over against the works of which a new and Holy Spirit is set, to enter into all hearts who listen to his pleas from without and open to His **direction**. Christ **Jesus** was the Holy Spirit incarnate. **Is** it strange, **then,** that He should **be** called to meet the unholy spirit; **yea,** incarnate, too, if you will?

But we shall not profit much over a study of the **form** in which the tempter came. **There** is a more important lesson for souls as interested as **ours.**

The devil came and found Jesus in **the** wilderness viewing the **work** of devastation about Him, and now within and upon Him. The earth barren, stones; the beasts, wild; the birds, shy; the man, hungry, faint, **friendless,** robbed **of all** power, dominion and fellowship. Jesus saw it, **felt it,** and must change it. How? Now **comes the devil.** "If thou be the Son of God, command these stones to become bread." *Command!* Is that **the** way to begin the work of redemption? *Command* these stones to become **bread!** Is that the **way to** rejuvenate **the** wilderness, **or. to** have man secure his bread? No, that is not **the way.** Then He will not assume it. But, **for His** own present needs, in **His** hunger, "Command!" **No, He** is not a master, but **a** servant. Let the Father command if He will, and what **He** will. The Son commands not. He lives **on** the word **of the Father.** He lives so as man, and for man. And so **He** speaks, "Man doth not live by bread alone, **but** by **every word** which proceedeth out of the mouth of God."

He had given up His ordinary resources. He had made Himself dependent. He, as the Son of God, with all power inherently, had come forth to tread the sphere of man, and live by the "Word of God." Life is not in bread; it is in God. That is simple—is it not? In His beautiful, simple trust it seemed so easy to say that. "Life is not in bread; you know that!" You have seen your dearest child pass out from your loving reach, while the cupboard was full, and the table unsparingly spread. Our neighbors and friends are dying around us, just while the bread carts are rattling over our streets with ten thousand loaves to meet the want. *Life is not in bread!* Poet, ring your changes on that trite saying that the sons of earth who know it well enough may feel it more and more! "Life is not in bread! *Life is in God!*" Songster, sing that in repeated strain from solo to full chorus, that the sons of men may hear it ringing in the soul! I speak thus unto you, "Not because ye know it not, but because ye know it." "Man doth not live by bread alone, but by every word of God."

Nor can the follower of Christ bring in the kingdom of eternal life to man, or restore the wilderness of earth to fertility and beauty by *commands*. How the blessed Jesus put that once to His own disciples, after His own temptations were all successfully resisted! "The kings of the earth exercise authority, but it shall not be so among you."

We have a sad story in the history of the Church where it has yielded to the tempter in this respect. In fact, I think the Church has met the tempter in history, in the very order of the lesson we study to-day. Its first great error was, it sought to sustain its own life, and that by authority. It spent years commanding stones to become bread; commanding dead souls to feed the life of the Church. The devil held a large place in theology, you know, for many years. I think it was because he had a large place in the Church. The poor, erring Church meant well. It was anxious to extend the kingdom. But the devil suggested an evil or unsuccessful way.

You all know there is enough in this one point for a whole sermon, and I cannot give time for the unfolding of it. The principal thoughts to bear ever with us are the two. The devil would have us seek our own life and subsistence first; and would have us seek it by demands or commands,—by the use of the divine prerogative. Christ repudiates both.

I feel how very needful it is for me to learn the lesson here. What a time this is for demanding our rights, for saying, "We must live," "We must have bread." What a temptation for the Church to be shouting, "You must keep up the Church." "The Almighty demands it of you. You must give a tenth or a fifth, or something, anyhow! If you don't, the Almighty will take it out of you!" What a temptation to the minister to say, "I must know the salary, and whether it is sure to be paid, and whether it is likely to be increased, before I enter upon my life of self-sacrifice in that region." My God and Saviour have mercy upon us, and teach us "Life is not in bread," nor does the kingdom of love make its onward march by the voice of authority or the clamor of demand! We shall move forward as we follow Jesus, and only as we follow Him. The minister, yes, and even the Church must get over its love of life and its fear of death. We must both be delivered from the love of all that makes life too sweet and death too terrible. We must lay down our lives, realizing that the Church that seeks to "save its life" shall "lose it." This Christ-spirit always prevailed in the days of outreaching and of growth. "Tribulation, famine, nakedness, peril, sword, none of these could separate the living and true followers from their work. When they had nothing to *save* they had everything to *give;* and great was the harvest or fruit thereof.

Now comes the tempter's second effort at misleading. *Misleading*, I say; for mark that he never seeks to check or to oppose. He is dealing with a willing and obedient spirit. He seeks, therefore, simply to misdirect it. He has tried the Saviour on the saving of His life, and finds Him willing to lose it, if necessary—if so the Father will. He now seeks to direct Him how to lose it, how to brave death, how to show His confidence in the word of His Father. Strange contrast. It reads, "Then the devil taketh Him into the holy city, and setteth Him on a pinnacle of the temple, and saith unto Him, If Thou be the Son of God, cast Thyself down: for it is written, He shall give His angels charge concerning thee," etc. Jesus had a heart burning with love for mankind. He had learned in His life that men did not understand the will, and purpose, and heart of His Father. They believed in His power, they knew He could throw down walls, as at Jericho; and divide rivers, as at Jordan. But all such manifestations of power did not command love, nor yet win hearts. His own spirit seemed to feel that the world would not be redeemed by any remarkable manifestations of peculiar physical or miraculous powers. What good would a leap from a temple pinnacle do? Whose sorrow would it alleviate, whose heart would it comfort? In what way could it be related to the regeneration of human hearts, or the construction or fulfilling of any holy purpose? He could do it. Yes, easily. And it would attract attention to Him? Yes. And it would win interest in Him? Yes. And it would give Him an earlier opportunity of being known? Yes. And then He could use all this influence in the extension of the Father's kingdom of love afterwards? Yes. That does seem logical. It is the world's logic. It is the tempter's philosophy. The world does feel an interest in the strongest muscle, in the swiftest speed, in the cleverest trick, in the loftiest genius, in the cutest wit, in the sweetest voice, in any and all of the arts which it delights to foster. Indeed, it is the world's effort at its own salvation. It believes in working from the outside. The devil keeps all his pious followers working along that line. It seems to be a good they are doing all the time. And that satisfies their conscience. But the world is made no better. Christ saw that. And if it were not the right way for man, it could be no personal use to Him. It would declare His wonderful confidence in His Father though? Yes, but it was not His *wonderful* confidence He wanted to declare, but it was His ordinary, His normal confidence. It was not a big faith He wanted to show, but a simple, living, and so-growing faith. Do you not remember how He taught this afterwards to His disciples? He did not say, "If ye had faith as this mountain, you could say to this mustard seed, Grow;"

but, "If ye had faith as the grain of mustard seed, you could say to this mountain, Move."

Christ rebuked the tempter. He did it for two reasons. First, it was not the method for the advancement of the kingdom of Heaven. Second, He did not personally want any advancement separate from that of the kingdom. To seek such, and expect divine support in reaching out for it, was not the path of faith. That would not be trusting the Father, but tempting the Almighty God.

I am sure you can see, on reflection, how the Church has always been so tempted in her history. I am sure you can see to-day how preachers and people representing the Church are similarly misled. I think there is no temptation so common to us in the pulpit. I am fearful that, if the power of the pulpit is waning anywhere, this is the reason. To men of God starting out with simple honest hearts, giving their lives to teach love, the appeal is made that they should "throw themselves," make the crowd notice them, catch their attention by art and man's device, and then they can "love them afterwards, and lead them unto God." To be a mountebank to-day, and an evangelist to-morrow; so tempts the devil sorely to-day. Or it may be that the world in our region is highly cultured and refined. Then the tempter pleads: "Climb to the highest pinnacle and gyrate there; make your best appeal to the things the world about you seeks for. This will secure your own success, and then you can work for the success of the cause." Now just look back. Jesus refused to do it. The people were looking for a king, for one come from God, a powerful one, one who could do as God did in the old days. They would go wild with joy if He would just show them that what they desired and delighted in, He possessed. Why did He not come and appeal to the art, and wisdom and "spirit of the age," and all that kind of thing we hear so much about to-day? Why not? It was not the manner of the propagation of the kingdom. That would be the very thing He taught His disciples not to do—not to parade even their best deeds. "Take heed that ye do not your alms before men, to be seen of them, otherwise you have no reward of your Father which is in heaven." So learned He, and taught, "The kingdom of God cometh not with observation."

I am sorry that I must leave this point of solemn warning, for it is freighted with important practical lessons for every honest worker in the vineyard of the Lord. But it is unfair to my subject not to refer to the third form of temptation from the devil.

"Again, the devil taketh Him up into an exceeding high mountain, and showeth Him all the kingdoms of the world and the glory of them ; and saith, All these things will I give Thee, if Thou wilt fall down and worship me." This was the most severe trial of all. It affected Him most to stand in the presence of all the valuable products of this great world ; to feel that they ought to be in the hands of the good and the true ; to feel deep down in the soul that they are really the children's own portion, of which they had been robbed by sin and error. Seeing the wicked flourish with them like the green bay tree, "not in trouble like other men," "not plagued like other men," was the reason for the old Psalmist saying, "My feet had well nigh slipped." The high mountains where we see the most glories are the slippery places, because we become so restless for our acquisition of the larger territory opened before us, that we lose our patience, and consequently our steadiness.

Jesus saw the kingdoms of this world ; He saw them not serving His Father, and so not attaining the true end of existence. He saw all the power going to waste, all the wisdom acting foolishly, all the capacities for true pleasure being surfeited with the base and sinful forms of delight. He wanted the kingdoms of this world for His Father. He came to secure them. It would take Him a long time to win them in His way. Here was the offer of them as a gift. Or here was the offer of the devil's help to secure them unto Him. Should He accept the easy way? He did not. Why? First, because it could not accomplish the work. Second, if it could, He would not let the devil take His crown. He came to "destroy the works of the devil," to rescue this world from his hands. He would make no compromises. He need not; He would abide His Father's will. "Not by might nor by power, but by My spirit, saith the Lord." It is written, Thou shalt worship, serve, obey, acknowledge, the Lord thy God— or thy God as the Lord, and Him only.

My time for application has gone. We will take it as a separate theme of study some day, if God spares us. Let us not be afraid, though, to cease our foolish compromises with the devil, and the world, and the flesh, and acknowledge only our God as the Master. If He cannot give us the lost dominion, depend upon it, no other can. But hark! I hear a song! Nay, it has died away again. Let us go back to Jesus standing upon the mountain-top. He has refused the offer of the tempter. The kingdoms of this world—the very desire of His all-redeeming love—which he longed to possess and give back to His redeemed children, whom He would have "inherit the earth"—all this He has refused, given up, sacrificed. But hark! I hear the song again! Listen! Yes, it comes, it grows, it swells upon the ear! I hear the tread also of a mighty host; and the song is filling all the universe with its sweeping air! Oh! hear it, hear it! He has the victory after all! "Hallelujah! Hallelujah! The kingdoms of this world have become the kingdoms of our God and of His Christ, and He shall reign forever and ever!" O follower of the meek and lowly, fear not the outcome of faith and submission! Question no more the wisdom, and power, and love of your Master, and follow Him on through conflict to victory.

LIFE IS NOT IN BREAD.

This beautiful poem was inspired under the preaching of the preceding sermon. The author of it sat in the congregation, and went home with the words ringing in his ears and heart, "Life is not in bread." It was afterwards presented to the pastor, who, with the author's consent, gives it now to the readers of this volume.   J. E. L.

LIFE IS NOT IN BREAD.

BY LLEWELLYN A. MORRISON.

Life is not in bread!
Famished ones, o'er all the earth,
Sorrow's baneful heirs from birth,
Ye, who struggle day by day,
Bitter burdens, scanty pay,
Serfs of famine's gaunt delay,
Hunger's brood surround the door;
Can ye reach your Master's lore?
It, alone, remains in store,
Rings it hope for evermore.
    Life is not in bread.

Life is not in bread!
Sheltered ones, who wisely toil,
Who from workshop, sea or soil,
Or the gifts which commerce sends,
Gain fruition's golden ends.
Make, with mammon's treasure, friends,
Let this truth have truest heed
(Soul of Nature's forceful creed),
Life hath higher source and need,
Than the fires the furrows feed.
    Life is not in bread.

Life is not in bread !
Throned ones, who reign as kings
High above earth's meaner things ;
Heirs of all the centuries' gain,
Scoffing want, and care, and pain,
Scorning labor's feudal stain,
Midst abundance crowned, at ease ;
Though the world-things charm and please,
They, no soul-pang can appease ;
Life remaineth not in these.
    Life is not in bread.

Life is not in bread !
Mortals all ! Attend the word,
'Tis the message of the Lord !
Still it rings above the din,
O'er the discord and the sin
Of the years, which have come in
Since it rang from Pisgah's slope,
Love's perennial horoscope,
Flashing time's eternal hope,
Where the sin-bound blindly grope.
    Life is not in bread.

Life is not in bread !
    'Tis in God.
Seek divorcement from the clod,
    Child of God !
Life hath source above the sod ;
    Lift thine eyes !
Wisdom's beacons flood the skies,

And her light
Pushes outward Error's night
And expands
Till its glory gilds the lands
And ascends;
While the mortal comprehends,
Life is but in God.

Life is but in God !
Every word
That proceedeth from the Lord,
Everywhere,
In the earth and in the air,
Rings the truth.
Pæon of immortal youth :
He, who bends a listening ear,
He may hear ;
She, who trains a vision, free,
She may see ;
All, who wisdom's lessons heed,
They may read ;
Who their love on truth bestow,
Each may know :
Life is but in God.

Life is but in God !
Shining stars, in whitest speech,
Nightly teach ;
Central suns, in dazzling rout,
Flash it out;

Circling planets, from their track,
  Flash it back;
Till, from universal plains
  And domains,
Comes to eye, and ear, and soul:
  From the whole,
  Life is but in God.

Life is but in God!
All the round earth's rhythmic rune
  Blends, in tune;
Every voice, in nature's throng,
  Joins the song;
Sonorous songsters, in the groves,
  Prompt their loves;
Billows, breaking on the shore,
  Evermore;
Zephyrs, whispering soft and low,
  As they go,
Balmy breezes, breathing rest
  To each breast;
Gusty gales, in troublous sweep
  O'er the deep;
Each, of all the rippling rills,
  As it trills;
Moon-kissed meadows, verdant vales,
  Daisy'd dales,
Waving woodlands, ferny fells,
  Dreamy dells,
Fragrant flowers, in rich perfume,
  And in bloom;

In their mystic native tongue
    All have sung ;
In their holy, God-known speech,
    Each doth teach :
" *Not in earth, where death is rife,*
    Dwelleth life ;
Life hath source above the sod,
    'Tis in God.
    Life is but in God."

    Life is but in God !
    Clearer still
Than the tuneful song-bird's trill,
Or the music of the rill,
    Or the voice
In which wold and fen rejoice,
Crooning nature's cheerful choice,
    Is the lore
From the garnered treasure-store
Of the *Book*, which, o'er and o'er,
Tells of life for evermore ;
Every promise points above,
Every warning limneth love ;
Every lesson leads to light,
Every statute to the right ;
All its precepts, through the days,
Quicken souls in wisdom's ways ;
All its testimonies shine
With a recompense, divine ;
All its laws, though stern and broad,
Bring to Christ, the Son of God ;

Its commandments keep and hide,
While its fulness hath supplied
Every good, by earth denied ;
All its righteous judgments lead
To the Judge of quick and dead;
All its sweet allurements bring
To the city of the King,
Pictured in Apocalypse ;
(Death and hell hath there eclipse)
Where the white robed ransomed call
From the glory, unto all :
" *Leave the sombre earth-life, dim,*
Seek eternal life through Him,
Christ, the God revealed, who died,
Whom the heavens hath glorified.
Whosoever will may come,
Dwell in an immortal home,
Have the life He hath, above ;
Love is life, and God is love,
    Life is but in God ! "

VI.
FORMING ATTACHMENTS.

"*And the two disciples heard Him speak, and they followed Jesus. Then Jesus turned, and saw them following, and saith unto them, What seek ye? They said unto Him, Rabbi, Where dwellest Thou? He saith unto them, Come and see.*"

JOHN i. 37, 38.

FORMING ATTACHMENTS.

IN our last lesson we beheld, with much satisfaction, the triumph of Jesus over those sources of temptation which it is the lot of humanity to share; and especially did we mark His conflict and victory as the great Redeemer of the human race. First, He must Himself not fall into the sins or errors which brought man to his degradation; second, He must not shrink from the severe and only method by which these are to be overcome in the race of which He is now the new member and Head. The scene of the wilderness has a pleasing conclusion, "Then the devil leaveth Him, and, behold, angels came and ministered unto Him." A welcome change! The very manner of the record strengthens our belief in the personalities of the unseen ones. The devil, the angels—the enemy, the friends. If the latter be real, so must be the former. Repudiate the personal enemy, and you repudiate the personal friends. Say there is no evil angel to tempt, and to be conquered, and to "leave Him," and then you must forfeit the record that good "angels came and ministered unto Him." The angels did not minister to Him in the conflict, but after it was over. He must not be spared the fulness of the self-sacrifice, but all He hath freely given should be graciously restored.

Once more, now, we find the Saviour moving forth to enter into the work of inoculating the race with the Life, of which He is the immortal germ. Again, we see Him apparently alone, and, one would think, almost bewildered where and how to begin. As we leave the wilderness with Him, we mark the simple, natural— divinely natural, I mean—trend of His pursuit. Is He to reveal His Father? Has He the law and the prophets—God-given and God-inspired—to fulfil? Has He the work of John the Baptist to complete? Then He will find John, and John's work, and John's disciples. Surely His work must begin there. We have been directed to the fourth Gospel for the details of His first work in this direction. The three other evangelists were not commissioned to write of this, because there was one who saw it all and was a party to its incidents. He is, therefore, fitly chosen to make the record.

It is really interesting and instructive beyond measure to watch how Jesus proceeds upon this tremendous undertaking. We have wondered already at His refusals of the suggestions in the wilderness to take what would seem to be the easy way, and what evidently would be our way, if we were taught no better. Did we learn last Sabbath what we must repudiate as worldly, as devilish, and, consequently, as futile and unavailing? Let us, then, follow Him with great care and learn what to adopt as heavenly, as divine, and, consequently, as fruitful and availing.

According to the record, we find that Jesus made His way to the banks of the Jordan river, where the Baptist was still pursuing his evangelistic labors with quite a school of disciples gathered around him. These disciples of the forerunner had evidently come from some distant points to attend his ministry, and many of them had become temporary dwellers in the region with their tents pitched along the banks of the river. The names appear in the narrative of some from the remote Galilee, seventy miles away. The reading of the context before us rather warrants our belief that Jesus Himself had secured a tent for a temporary abiding place, and probably by the multitude would be taken for one of John's disciples.

About this time, some members of the Jewish officiary, roused by the stir which John's preaching had brought about, felt it necessary to question John upon the purport and end of his mission. "Priests and Levites," it is written, "were sent to ask him, Who art thou?" He said he was not the Christ. And then they asked, "Art thou Elias?" And he said, "No." And they inquired, "Art thou that prophet?' And he said, "No." Then they proposed the question, "What sayest thou of thyself?"

Now, John felt that he was not sent to bear witness of himself. He had really nothing to say about himself. That, indeed, was one of the strong features of his whole ministry. So now, in answer to the pointed question, "What sayest thou of thyself?" he answers, "I am the voice of one crying in the wilderness, Make straight the way of the Lord." That was no new information. They all knew that to be just what he was. It may have been news to them when he added, "as said the prophet Esaias." For had they been good students of their own Scriptures, they should have known that "they were they which testify of him."

Listening to the words of John, we are clearly convinced that he was "preparing the way of the Lord." It was quite orderly, then, that Jesus should come that way. And just as John was bearing, next day, this faithful witness, he seeth Jesus coming among others to the service; and he looked around upon priests, Levites, strangers, and his own devoted disciples, and pointing to Jesus, said: "Behold the Lamb of God, which taketh away the sins of the world. This is He of whom I said, After me cometh a man which is preferred before me, for He was before me." Following this, John gave unquestionable evidence of the truth of his own mission, and also of the testimony from above to the person of Jesus as the Messiah.

And still John went on preaching, but now he added the testimony with the exhortation. And Jesus waited, retiring to His tent like the rest of the disciples in the evening. Life must wait for the development of the media. There must be no forcing, no undue pressure. Any such abnormal process would leave a mark of imperfection on the result, on the beautiful flower and fruit. "The kingdom of God is as though a man did plant seed in the ground."

Again the next day John seeth Jesus. This time two of the Baptist's disciples were with him talking, doubtless, of the truth dear alike to him and them. As Jesus passed by, John said, "There is the Lamb of God." On hearing these words, the two disciples left John and followed after Jesus. He had not sought to impress them in any way by the powers of sense. But these two follow Him. Right, right! These two were ready. They were John's most advanced pupils. John's mission had been perfected in them. Their very hearts were keyed up to the point where a passing Christ could touch them and draw them unto Himself. John had so well taught them that they were not unwilling to leave his class for the higher one. He had taught them on purpose for the higher class and its teacher. He had led them to believe that there would be somebody to teach them greater things than he knew. Oh, that was wise teaching. I wish more of us could learn it. So when the teacher came they were ready to "forget the things behind and reach forward." Hence, seeing Jesus, they followed after Him. It is natural; I mean, it is divine.

"Then Jesus," it is said, "turned and saith unto them, What seek ye?"

How marvellous it is; marvellously simple! Jesus out in the world bringing life for man; men seeking for that very life which Jesus is bringing them! They meet, they coalesce. "Rabbi, where dwellest Thou? Where dost Thou teach? Where can we sit at Thy feet? We are Thy disciples; Thou art our Rabbi." "Were dwellest thou?" "Come and see!" there need be no delay; I need not tell the place I dwell and put the visit off. "Come and see!" Come now! "And the went in and abode with Him that day." They met never to part again. They met in the Eternal Spirit. The seeking two knew not all it meant. It was the sunrise of love. It was the divinely created want finding the divinely furnished supply.

But there was another significance about it. It was the first point of contact between Jesus Christ the Redeemer and the life of the human race. He had fastened His life grip upon the spirit of humanity in the taking of these two ready hearts into the fellowship of His own heart of love. How we almost feel like applauding Andrew and that companion of his, who, though unnamed here, was doubtless the beloved writer of this Gospel! The dear faithful souls and disciples of the truth. How much we owe them for being ready to receive the Lord when He came that way! For only to such as could "receive Him" was He able to give "power to become the sons of God."

Let us stay a little while at this point, and learn a lesson or two. We are thoroughly aware that the whole Jewish Church, and indeed a many of other race and creed, were eagerly looking for and desiring the coming of a Messiah. We recognize, also, that John the Baptist accepted it as his mission to prepare the way, and announce the coming of the same. It is significant therefore, that his announcement was couched in no such terms as would meet the form of desire prevalent in the popular mind. It was not the popular Saviour, Christ came to be. To usher in the true Saviour, John must preach repentance, must denounce sin and sinners, and gather about him those who felt the truth of his words, and were prepared to renounce evil, and love God and goodness. This was what John called preparing the way for the Saviour. Then he announces the Saviour, not as a king of nations, not as a royal potentate, not as a warrior in battles, not as a party leader, not as the priest of a sect; but in terms strange indeed to the multitude, but congruous enough to the disciples who had heard and obeyed: "Behold the Lamb of God, which taketh away the sins of the world."

This form of introduction takes the Christ out of all the temporal and worldly atmosphere in which His reputed people, the Jews, were generally looking for him. "The Lamb of God!" What does it mean, you ask. O brethren, don't ask. I cannot tell you all. It means all you and I can make it mean, and then more for every other student or disciple. Let one see in these words a reference to Abraham's sacrifice, and the prophetic utterance, "God will provide Himself a lamb for a burnt-offering." Let another see a reference to the awful night in Egypt, when the death angel passed through, and the people of God took a lamb and sprinkled the blood upon the lintel of the door; and, where it was seen a lamb had been slain, the angel of death passed by. Let another see in it the hero of

Isaiah's vision, who was "led as a lamb to the slaughter and as a sheep before her shearers, as dumb, yet who opened not His mouth." Let another see only the reference to the morning and evening sacrifice of every day ; and another note its signification in the Passover lamb, which was the marked figure of the important annual feast. Or let another see only the meek, pure, innocence of the Lamb, and behold this as the meaning of John's reference. Let all see, let all tell what they see in "the Lamb of God." Let us each bring our visions, and our thoughts, and our ideas, and our truths, and add them to the others. This is the way to build up the temple of the truth. We must not bring our ideas to *substitute for* others, but to *add to* others. This poor world, even of religion, is mortally bare of truths ; just because, in the past, every mind which had received a worthy conception, or formed a worthy ideal, must find a place for it in the great pantheon only by dethroning some other, just as worthy, from its seat. There is room for all our scanty thoughts, yes, and all our most sublime inspirations ; yes, and room for all the others, too. Let us be rich, not poor ; let us save each others' thoughts, not destroy them. They all help to the perfect knowledge of the truth.

I have been much struck with the power of these words of the Baptist on the disciple which he now had transferred to Jesus. To John, I mean now the disciple John, the words "Lamb of God" were just right. It brought the next truth to his hungry soul. And somehow forever after he saw Jesus as a "Lamb." He found Jesus so easy to love. He was the only disciple who could be free to fondle Jesus. And when he drew out his apocalyptic visions for us to read, we see how often, and above all other scenes, he beheld Jesus as a "Lamb in the midst of the throne." And it was so also with the first words of Jesus to John. They struck deep; they found the very bottom of his heart. He never forgot them. That generous invitation, "Come and see!" Ever and anon that face and that voice haunted him with "Come and see!" There was always some new *where* to come. There was always some new *beauty* to see. Through all Christ's sojourn on earth, John was ready to come to His side and see. After the public addresses, delivered in parable to the curious and promiscuous crowd, John would come to the Teacher when alone, and say, "Tell us the parable," and so it is recorded that "when they were alone He expounded all these things to His disciples." Especially do we find in the writings of John that Jesus was the solution of every problem to him. It is John who tells us that Jesus is the Truth, the Light, the Logos, the Way, the Life—the one Being who could say to every asking, inquiring, seeking soul, "Come and see!"

When John saw in the Patmos vision that in the right hand of Him that sat upon the throne there was a sealed book; and it was found that no man in heaven or earth was able to open it and look therein, John wept. He was very anxious to know the mysterious writing there. Then, when the news came that "the Lion of the tribe of Judah," had prevailed to open the book, John says, "I beheld, and lo, in the midst of the throne among the elders and the four beings stood the Lamb. And he came and took the book out of the right hand of Him that sat upon the throne; and I saw the Lamb open one seal, and one of the beings said for Him, "Come and see!" And when He had opened the second seal, the second being said, "Come and see!" and so with the third and fourth beings that spoke for the Lamb who opened the book. The word was "Come and see!"

And it is such a simple, reasonable word. It is so much more divine than all the excruciating ways we have of trying to lead man from darkness to light, and sin to holiness. "Come and see!" Not "Stand back and believe!" No pressure upon the undeveloped mind or heart, no impossibilities to perform, no abnormal steps to pursue. "Come and see!"

And this is Christ's way to the incoming kingdom. The kingdom will come to the heart, and mind, and frame of man just as fast as he "comes and sees." It is the comers and seers which are the "Salt of the earth" and the "light of the world." Christ took little cognizance, from the kingdom's standpoint, of the crowds that followed Him to see His miracles, or eat of His loaves, or to hope for His political interference to their good. He counted as His work His dealings with those who came to His retirement to *see*. This is the true work everywhere. It is not how many thousands did John Wesley and his preachers address in the fields, and lanes, and amphitheatres, but how many came aside afterward to see. Our great work is not in our public popularity, but in our power to call aside, and our power to make the disciples to see. Our class-meetings and their work tell how the kingdom among us grows. It is so in the communion classes and inquiry services of other branches of the Christian Church. And in our churches to-day it is the ones— be they many or few—who come to see, to see the truth, who come on purpose to penetrate some deeper mystery, or find some hidden pearl yet to be brought to light, who are the real members of the kingdom. This outside hanging on, lazily avowing our belief in the "concern," and our "belonging" to it in a way, because we have allowed them to put down our name to please them and swell their numbers, is utterly unworthy any mention in so real, and true, and pure, and perfect a building as the erection of a spiritual kingdom with the pure, perfect, simple, plain, unhiding Christ for its Head and for its Life.

Let us get this lesson from our study to-day. We must have learners—anxious, seeking ones. We must feed them well with the truth. Be they only two, or four, or twelve, they are worth more to Christ and to His kingdom in the earth than all the selfish, vacillating crowd that follow on sensation's wing. But we dare not call the seeking ones aside to see, unless we have something to show them, something plain, something they can see. Christ forced nothing on Andrew or John. What they went to see they saw. And what they saw they were able to tell; we will mark now in what way they sought to tell it.

We resume the reading of the record. How important it seems now to us, for we are seeking the path to the world's redemption. We are reading how Jesus Christ went about the winning of the human race back to His Father's rule and fellowship. The fortieth verse reads, "One of the two . . . which followed Him was Andrew, Simon Peter's brother." He first findeth his own brother Simon, and saith unto him, We have found the Messias, and he brought him to Jesus."

Andrew knew where to go. He knew that Simon was one who sought the Messias. Hence the joy of saying, "We have found." All these disciples of the Baptist should be very susceptible to the presence and power of Jesus. Yet all were not so. It was no fault of the teacher, though; they were slow to learn, because they were not intense seekers. But Andrew found Simon; and some think John found Philip, though, as the writer here, he withholds his own name and work. And then Philip found Nathanael. These were all ready to receive Christ. These were all well taught of the Baptist, and were devoted to God and His kingdom as best they knew it.

Now, you can see how the kingdom is being built up by the gathering together of those that are nearest to it. The whole system of the revelation of the Father from the beginning is seen to be of one mind, and the parts fit into each other, or, at least, seem to grow into or out of the other. We can understand that beautiful prayer of Jesus recorded by John, who knew so well its meaning, because he had been with Him from the beginning. Remember, from your reading of the seventeenth chapter, how Jesus prayed over His work, and said to His Father, "I have manifested

Thy name unto the men which Thou gavest Me; Thine they were, and Thou gavest them Me, and they have kept Thy word." Jesus chose the best, purest, most devoted children that His Father had on earth with which to begin the kingdom, as it were, anew, among men. You can see now why He put His prayer in that beautiful order of procedure. "I pray for them, I pray not for the world" (first) "but for them which Thou hast given Me. I pray not that they should be taken out of the world, but that they be kept from the evil. Sanctify them through Thy truth. Thy word is the truth." Then He proceeds, "Neither pray I for these alone, but for them also which shall believe on Me through their word." I pray that they may come into the same fellowship. "As Thou, Father, art in Me and I in Thee, that they also may be one in us." And I pray this that "the world may believe that Thou has sent Me." The prayer reached to the world, you see, all right enough. The end of all the prayer for the disciples and followers, for their sanctification, and unity, and fellowship, is "that the world may believe." But He said, "I pray not for the world," first. The world must see, and hear, and be impressed before it can believe that Jesus came forth from God. So Jesus prayed, because so Jesus had been led of the Spirit from the beginning. He perceived that this is the way to extend the kingdom of God in the earth.

We have spoken of Andrew finding first his own brother. We hear little of Andrew in the history of the Church. But he brought to the Church his brother Peter. And we hear much of Peter. The quiet fidelity of Andrew gave birth to the wide usefulness which is connected always with the name of his brother. It was quite reward enough for Andrew to be called "Simon Peter's brother," and to feel that he had been able in any way to contribute to his brother's knowledge of Jesus and the kingdom. Philip, it is said, was of the same city as Andrew and Peter; and to me it is somewhat interesting to think that they all came from a northern town of Galilee, called "Galilee of the Gentiles." Somewhat significant, I say, that Jerusalem, with all its Priests, and Scribes, and Levites, with all its ritual, and pomp, and paraphernalia of worship, should not be able to furnish one of the first disciples to greet the long-expected Messiah, the hope of Israel, and the Saviour of the world.

There can be no thought more prominent in viewing this lesson to-day than the constructive character of Jesus' work. He began quietly to build, to gather, to construct. And when His disciples came to Him, He added something to them. He did not ask them to give up anything, but to take something. What He gave to Andrew and John on the night they abode with Him is not recorded. But could they go forth next day to say, "We have lost?" Oh, no! but we have "found" something, a treasure indeed. When Simon came he received a new name. The ambitious spirit which Peter had, the Saviour was not to destroy, but to fulfil, *i.e.*, to put to its right use; so He opened a future of promise to Simon which fastened him at once to the kingdom. When Nathanael came, He cheered him with an honest eulogy, "An Israelite, indeed, in whom there is no guile." If what Jesus said were true, and it must have been, it could not injure any cause to say it. Nathanael knew himself if he was pure and honest in his desires and heart. He may often have been misapprehended, as the purest are wont to be, in this uncharitable world; and it would be precious to feel that at least one heart knew the honesty of his purposes. Nathanael answered, "Whence knowest Thou me?" Jesus answered, "Before that Philip called thee, when thou wast under the fig tree, I saw thee." Oh, how simple a teacher! Why didn't He say, "I know all things and everybody, and all they think, and speak, and do?" That would be destructive. Too much light at once is as ruinous as too little. He wanted just to tell them what they could, without unreasonable effort, understand. So He said to Nathanael, "I saw you in your secret place of prayer under the fig tree." And Nathanael blushed to think his privacy had been invaded. But if Jesus saw his praying place and heard him pray, He knew a good deal about Nathanael. And so Nathanael responded from his guileless soul, "Rabbi, Thou art the Son of God; Thou art the King of Israel." And Jesus must add a little more to such a confession of faith. He can build a little further on such a foundation. "Because I said unto thee I saw thee under the fig tree, believest thou? Thou shalt see greater things than these."

Such a power of belief will see beyond the common ken. "Come and see!" "Verily, verily, I say unto you, hereafter," or after a while, with a growing faith, "you shall see heaven open and the angels of God ascending and descending upon the Son of Man." And you look up at me now, and say what did he mean by that. I can never tell you. That was for the guileless and believing Nathanael. If you have a faith like his you will have something to see that is worthy. That vision means that Nathanael with his faith should see what the rest of us cannot understand when it is written down as it is here. That is a prize sure only to such a seeing eye.

My dear fellow students, does not the precious record unfold to our seeking souls. This whole morning we have been watching the Saviour forming attachments and becoming a larger self in other selves. The work begins, the race is being saved. The kingdom is coming. Oh, the value of ready hearts, of seeking spirits, of teachable minds! Christ's first question to humanity in the persons of Andrew and John was, "What seek ye?" In the name of Jesus I ask it of you to-day. You are here, following Him. I speak to you as His followers, "What seek ye?" May I be sure I hear you say, "Rabbi, where dwellest Thou? Where teachest Thou? Where can I sit at Thy feet and learn? Thou art my Rabbi, I am Thy disciple." If this be thy true answer to-day, and always, then to thy out-looking, longing spirit comes the welcome words, "Come and see!" It comes in every new morning and evening mercy; it comes in every changing experience; it comes in the darkness and in the light. Come, do not stay; it is a call forward; on from pleasure or the toil of yesterday to the new joy and duty of the morrow; on from the old lesson well learned and proven, to the new one full of interest as yet unsolved; on from the knowledge in part, and the prophecy in part, to that which is perfect and entire, wanting nothing. "Come and see!" Now we see but in dim lines a many things;

now we see men as trees walking; now we see through a glass darkly. "Come and see!" Thy vision shall become clearer, and thy prospect shall widen to a vast expanse, till thine eye shall "see the King in His beauty;" and the land that is afar off shall become nigh, for the kingdom of God is come.

VII.

AT THE MARRIAGE.

"*And the third day there was a marriage in Cana of Galilee; and the mother of Jesus was there: and both Jesus was called, and His disciples to the marriage.*"

JOHN ii. 1, 2.

AT THE MARRIAGE.

OUR last meditation on the earthly life of the Son of God left us watching Him "forming attachments" with the children of men. On the banks of the Jordan, from the number of John's disciples, He had found the fellowship of five, who voluntarily clung to Him as their "Rabbi" or Master. Andrew, Simon, John, Philip and Nathanael were His first associates. These had all evidently come from the northern part of the country, roused by the preaching of the Baptist that the kingdom was nigh at hand. It was because they were "seekers" that they found so soon their way into the kingdom.

In following the record as given by one of this number, we are led to watch them move away from the scenes of the evangelist to the region of their own homes. Their fellowship with John the Baptist was completed, it was fulfilled. They had found the Lord of whom John was the herald. In them the herald's work was accomplished. They could, therefore, consistently say farewell to John, and go henceforth where Jesus should be.

But where would Jesus be? The Baptist had made his abode in the wilderness, and his mode of life was severe, lonely, ascetic.

It is interesting and profitable to know that Jesus did not confine His disciples to the seclusion of life which John had manifested. The Baptist's was a life which harmonized in its unfolding with the truths he felt and declared. He spent his life in fasting and prayer for the sins of the people and nation. John emphasized *sin;* Jesus should emphasize *salvation*. John came to announce an overhanging judgment unto *death*, and to declare a coming deliverer; Jesus came to be the giver of *life* to every one who sought or desired it. Life was His staple blessing. It was the one thing needed for a dying world.

It will be interesting, as we move forward in the blessed study, to find that it was Life He imparted on all occasions of His ministration. Did He heal the eyes of the blind? Blind eyes are simply dead eyes— eyes in which the vital force is weak or wanting; and so He gave life to dead eyes. Did He heal the ears of the deaf? In like manner it was simply giving life to dead ears. Did He heal the withered hand? A withered hand is only a dead hand; He gave unto it life. Did He make five loaves feed five thousand bodies? This was only giving "more abundant" life to that which possessed some. And so all through, in His physical realm of ministration.

Did He come with a new law, or a new commandment? No, but just to put life into the old, so it could grow unto fulfilment. He came to fulfil every jot and tittle of the law, and His new commandment was the one they had possessed "from the beginning." To the realm of "the truth" He came, saying, "I am come that ye might have life."

We see Him moving forth, then, into the world of energies and forces, to be Himself a force to make all things new. To get old means to lose the life forces, and to begin decay. He came to make all things young, fresh, alive, that they should unfold the beauties to which they had never yet matured.

He was a life-force, an inspiration, to His disciples, as they journeyed along together. Those five men never felt so much alive as they did when Jesus was with them. There was life in His presence, and life in His words, and life in His looks, and life in His tones; there was always life emanating from Him to those who believed upon Him, and who could therefore receive it.

Our lesson to-day finds Him among His own friends

and those of His disciples. He is once more in the company of His mother. How glad she would be to see Him! To see Him in His new capacity as a consecrated teacher, (how much more she hardly knew yet), for the nation, and the world. To us who are students, He must stand out as the central figure in any group, His word, His deed, will be the important issue in every fellowship.

"There was a marriage in Cana of Galilee, and the mother of Jesus was there: and both Jesus was called and His disciples to the marriage." This was only the third day after Jesus and the disciples found each other. It would take all this time for them to make the journey from the Jordan valley, where they had been in the company of the Baptist. This was, therefore, the first stopping place and the first event of importance in the life of Jesus with His disciples. We may well conclude that the principals in this marriage were congenial spirits with Mary and Jesus and His disciples. Also, we would think they were of a class of society in rank about the same.

Jesus did not, then, make His first appearance in uncongenial surroundings. We have reason to be glad that this record is given us by the writer John. The other evangelists have placed Jesus at once amid scenes of sin and wretchedness. Verily he had a place there, and a place becoming His ministry to the relief of sorrow and trouble. But religion is not only to be placed as an offset for sorrow and death. It is to minister to life, and gladness, and truth, wherever such abides. It is not to be as a "lamp burning at the door of a sepulchre," but as a sunshine upon all the true joys and happinesses of human life. The first fellowship is at a wedding. He lends His first presence at the inauguration of new home. "There is no place like home;" no place so human, no place so divine. Let this be a standing protest against any one, in the name of Christ, making it a virtue to abstain from marriage. It is the source of all human relations and the nursery of all true affections. It is used to symbolize "the mystical union betwixt Christ and His Church," because of the truth that is potent in the symbol itself. These very five disciples were the first-fruits of Christ's own love, and the augury of that marriage which is finally to be celebrated when the redeemed " Bride " shall be "adorned for her husband." The same John which attended with Him at this wedding, saw, with holy inspiration, in after years the nuptials of the Lamb and His Bride as she was beheld "coming down out of heaven " as the " New Jerusalem."

Looking at the matter in this simple way, it seems the most natural of all things that Christ's first public manifestation of Himself should be in connection with a marriage.

I have already spoken of the fact that this company was doubtless one of spiritual congeniality. Unless there was a large element of honest piety among the principals and their relatives, such persons of guileless repute as Mary and Jesus and Nathanael (who was of this very Cana) would not have been the invited guests. This is, then, another evidence that Jesus, like a wise sower, sought for the good ground in which to cast His seed. It is a further proof of what we taught in our lesson on "Forming attachments," that it is the wisdom of God to use all the good there is in the world as its "salt" and its "light."

The coming Son of God would not despise the Father's true seekers after Him, but indeed hasten first to find them and claim them as the best ones to aid Him in the establishment of His kingdom. Certainly the kingdom of God comes ready to receive men at their best, not at their worst; and to gather into its treasury of grace not the wrecks of human life, but the rich spoils of its youth and strength, its intellect and beauty. Nor are we to suppose that Jesus was unable to share joy with the innocently merry and joyous. He who came to turn earth's sorrows into joy must have delighted, indeed, to find some joy upon earth to share. If the law of Christian sympathy is written, "Rejoice with them that do rejoice, and weep with them that weep," we may not look in vain through the life of the Christ for the place of rejoicing, as well as for the record that "Jesus wept."

And the most natural place for rejoicing is at a marriage. Perhaps you have thought it was a freak of sinful humanity that led the bride to deck herself with jewels and wear her brightest and best robes at the altar of Hymen. But, if so, you are greatly mistaken. It is supremely consistent. It is in harmony with God's provision, everywhere that our eyes can read His will. Nature is full of it. When does the lowest lichen that clings to the wall reveal its brighest color? When does the lowly moss assume its richest green and put on its orange capsules? When do all plants display their most gorgeous color of leaf and blossom? Read carefully your botany and you will learn that it is in the nuptial hour. When does the dull crawling caterpillar blossom into a blazoned butterfly? When does the glow-worm trim its tiny lamp? When does the richer crimson come upon the robin's breast? It all comes in the season that the insect and the bird alike seeks its mate. This is also the season of music; for the forests that are silent during all other seasons, wake up to rapture of song for the marriage of the birdal tribe. I just mention this to impress you that it is not the fashion of Paris, or London, or New York which rules the marriage festivities; but it is a divinely implanted law or instinct which brings its best to serve the consummation of love. Oh, what a feast it will be when the Son of God shall bring in His Bride, when the Creator Father will bring on His fulness, and the marriage of the Lamb shall be accomplished. I want to be there. I want you to be there. We are invited guests. Let us make our calling sure.

Let us come now to certain incidents in connection with this festive occasion, one of which finds particular mention.

The customary wine was insufficient to meet the wants of the company. This to those who sought to entertain the guests was quite a misfortune. The record tells us that the mother of Jesus came to Him and declared, "They have no wine." To this Jesus responded, "Woman, what have I to do with thee? Mine hour is not yet come." These words in their uttered form to us seem to carry a severity which we cannot believe they were intended to convey. They are not according to our vernacular. This has led to a great variety of interpretations for them. There is no possible shadow of ill-respect in the use of the term "woman," and it is a broader term than "mother," any way. "Mother" is a precious term between two individual hearts, known to each other by the fond relationship. But Jesus had assumed the higher and broader relation to all human creatures, and He loved Mary now because she was a woman—and a good one, too—better than because she was His mother.

"What have I to do with thee?" Many opinions have been expressed upon the meaning of these words. I can simply add mine. I have not tried to form it. It just reads to me this way:—Why should *you* come to Me for help? Why should they ask *you* to ask *Me?* Why not ask Me themselves? Why should I not be approachable? What have I to do with you in this matter? When the time comes I will deal with the servants. Let them come to Me if there is anything to be done.

It seems to me rather like a kind, yet necessary, rebuke, not of the mother's generosity of intercession, but of that apparent feeling of need that her mediation was required. So, when she returned from speaking with Him, she said to the waiting servants, "Whatsoever He saith to you, do it." He will deal directly with *you*, He wants to do so. Be not afraid to speak with Him freely.

The keen perception of Him who "knew what was in man" beheld, we think, the first dawning of that error which has assumed large proportions in later years, that the mother of Jesus must stand between the suppliant and His great heart; and He would seek to arrest that error at its inception. He would have the way open for all of us to come directly to Himself with all our needs, and He would gladly supply them all according to His Father's will.

And He would also teach both Mary and us that He came not to be owned by one mother exclusively, or to be appropriated by a few brothers and sisters because they were her children, or to be limited to one household; but that everywhere men and women who should be willing to forget or to forsake father and mother, wife and children, houses and lands, that they should become sons and daughters of the Lord God Almighty, the same should be His "mothers, and sisters, and brethren." It is the lower law carried upward to the spiritual realm, and it is a consistent lesson, indeed, to be learned at a marriage feast, for it is written in nature as well as in the word, "Therefore shall a man forsake father and mother and cleave unto his wife, and they twain shall be as one flesh." He must now seek his own "Bride" and cling unto her till the consummation of love shall come in the "sweet by-and-by."

We read the whole record in our Scripture lesson.

The water pots stood in their wonted place. The servants were bidden to fill them, which they did. The command was now given, "Draw out, and bear unto the governor of the feast," which command was obeyed. The governor and, doubtless, others drank thereof; but it is written, "He knew not whence it was." It is important that we mark here the quiet, unostentatious way in which the deed of wonder was wrought. There was no stoppage in the movement of the festivities. There was no obvious crisis. There was no call to order, that all might see the wonder-working power displayed. Somehow we miss here the very thing for which the most of us have been taught to look. There was no effort to excite the surprise or even the attention of the company. Evidently the design was not unto that end. And I think that we ought to learn that the attitude in which we have placed the Saviour as doing mighty works for the special purpose of proving His divine authority and power, is one which He never really assumed. His aim, as to method, seemed to be along the lines of kindness, love, forgiveness, sacrifice, forbearance, and especially of ministration. And where there was belief to be strengthened, or need to be met, He used such powers as He judiciously could to accomplish the desired end.

By no display, however, could such a kingdom as

His be planted and builded up. The more this is studied, the more impressive the subject is. His kingdom "came not by observation." The Rev. Dr. McMillan, in speaking on the subject of the quietness of God's working, says, "The divine law of secrecy applies to all the institutions of God's kingdom. We know not how the Bible grew to completeness as the inspired Word of God, how the canon of either the Old or New Testaments was formed under the guidance of God's providence. We cannot tell how the Lord's Day came to supersede the Jewish Sabbath, and to establish itself as an essential part of the Gospel dispensation, for there is no formal enactment of it in the New Testament. So, too, with the sacraments of the Church, the signs and seals of God's kingdom, they all come not with observation. We cannot separate between the Jewish Passover and the Christian Communion, or indicate when the one rite merged into the other in our Lord's Supper in Jerusalem. The sacrament of infant baptism is not definitely mentioned and formally presented in the New Testament; although the rite very early took its place as an accepted element of the Christian organization. All these institutions are like a seed cast into the ground, which germinates and grows up, man knoweth not how."

And so around and about us in a constancy and regularity that fairly hide the potency, the blessings of God steal upon us. We sit at our festal boards daily and partake of the Father's bounties and, like the governor at the Cana feast, know not whence they are. All the while new blessings too are bursting out upon us, which, when we realize them we wonder, because we had not noticed their coming. For days, or months, or years they had been preparing, they had been unfolding, they had been perfecting for us. How our ideas pass from one form into another! We wake up with surprise to find ourselves believing things so very different now from our younger days. Yet we cannot tell the day and hour we sat down and exchanged the one form of belief for another. The most of us know little, indeed, of how, and when, and where our greatest treasures are wrought out for us and sent to us.

But was there no one at that feast who knew the source of this rich supply? Yes! There is a very significant statement here. It is enclosed within a parenthesis, and has a little completeness about itself. It is just such a word as John would have whispered to a few while he rehearsed the general story to the multitude. It reads, "But the servants which drew the water knew." Yes, that is a secret only a few know.

This is ever the servants' reward. The governor and the guests may sit and enjoy, but it is not the greatest honor always. "Which is the greater," once asked the Saviour, "he that serveth, or he that sitteth at meat?" And they answered Him, "Verily, he that sitteth at meat." Then said He, "Behold, I am among you as he that serveth!" Congruous with that He at another time taught them, "He that would be chief among you, let him be your servant." Oh, my dear helpers, do ye not know what this meaneth? "The servants which drew the water knew." The ones that helped Him, that heard His command, and did it, they knew. It is the workers that know how the blessings come. It is the teachers in the Sunday-school who have the truths to carry to others, who come to know their origin. It is those who read for others, think for others, care for others, run errands of mercy for others, these know. The giver of a cup of cold water is more than the receiver. It is the difference between the Saviour and the saved. The one who stands and ministers food, or silver, or clothing to the shivering beggar brother or sister at the door, is better than the one that receives it. It is the difference between the Saviour and the saved. "It is doing the will that knows the doctrine." "The servants that drew the water knew."

Ignorant and stupid as I am, I am sometimes greeted with the remark: "I don't see how you get all your beautiful ideas, where do they come from?" I'll tell you all to-day. I draw the water and bear it to you. That explains it to you. I can tell you no more. You must draw water and bear it forth to others. It was only water when they drew it, it changed to wine in the servants' hands.

In the treatment of this subject, it seems necessary in our day to make some inquiry into the alleged inconsistency of Jesus making wine for his guests. The sad abuse of the wine-cup has brought such sorrow to the sons and daughters of men that thousands who worship the Christ sit bewildered before the record. And what to them seems worse, the enemies of temperance claim Christ as their champion, and paint Him a central figure in their intoxications, ministering to them the sparkling beverage.

I have already, a few weeks ago, given you my own reading of this incident in my address to you on "The Bible and Prohibition,"* and I shall not, therefore, enlarge upon it again. I may, however, say that whatever need might appear to the prophetic eye of the Saviour for a change in the estimate of such beverages,

---

* See the remarks on this subject, page 161.

He would seek to bring about that change, not abruptly, but naturally. To that company of pious souls, their wine was an innocent refreshment. He would not seek to destroy their festive hour by shocking their moral senses with a conviction of wrong-doing. If there was a better truth for their good hearts to know, it should come upon them in such a way as to commend itself to their belief, and then to their practice.

I have already said to you on this matter, that I do not believe that, in the ordinary sense, and in the sense of our defenders of intoxicants, Jesus made any wine at all. To me there is a very important significance in the way in which He repudiated the *wine bottles*, and the way in which He emphasized and blessed the water. There are only two places where this miracle is mentioned, and in both of these it is said, with peculiar fidelity to the use of water, "he made the *water* wine."

I have spoken this morning how that every ministration of Jesus Christ was a ministration of life. To me this was such. It was the added "life" to the water borne in the hands of the servants that made it to the drinkers wine. Two things were accomplished by this method of procedure. He met the exigencies of the occasion without a question arising to disturb the freedom of the festivities. He so did it as to exalt and honor the pure and sparkling water, and to teach to those who should afterwards study His works in the light of the highest good unfolding to a growing race, that a glass of water, with the blessing of Christ upon it, is the best wine at the feast.

I shall not say any more upon this topic now. You are all familiar with the lesson this method of the Saviour's dealing brings to my own mind. It is difficult for me to speak from any other standpoint than my own reading.

Let us go from our study of this morning with glad hearts. We have seen how Jesus enters into our joys, and lends His aid to inspire them. Let us remember how He loves our marriage altars and sets His seal upon them. Of course, they must be true, real, pure, to have His presence and blessing. The home that is established only in the pride of wealth, or in social convenience, or in heated lust, He could not sanction with His presence.

Let us learn, also, to do our work in His name without ostentation, and find that the sweet order of nature will prove that Nature's God is ours; and if we

"—trust the All-Creating voice,
  Even faith desires no more."

Let us plant our seeds of truth and duty, and keep

the sun-rays of love upon the hearts that hold them, and "wait patiently for the Lord, and He shall give the desire of our hearts." Jesus wrought not for show, not to capture or convince unbelievers, but to confirm faith and love. Where unbelief was, no such works could be wrought. To Him that believeth, the blessings come.

VIII.
THE BIBLE AND PROHIBITION.

"Art thou for us, or for our adversaries?"
JOSHUA v. 13.

THE BIBLE AND PROHIBITION.

THERE are important moments in every life, moments on which whole destinies hinge. One false step has led into irrecoverable disgrace. One noble effort has secured an advantage which no foe could take away. It is the same with communities as it is with individuals. There are times of crisis. We are fast approaching one now. When, a few years hence, the scroll of history is unrolled, and our children read the record of the march and triumph of liberty, and truth, and temperance, and virtue; the name of this land and, we trust, of this year, shall occupy an important place. Fewer than we suppose are those who are not being aroused to the greatness of present issues.

There are some dull and sleepy souls who have not care enough to arouse them to enthusiasm. "They have eyes but see not, ears have they but they hear not, hearts they have, but cannot understand."

But these surely cannot be great in number. After

all the local agitations, and all the contests on platform, in press, and at the poll; after all the appeals of the oppressed, and the prayers of the toiling seekers after righteousness, which have filled our land during the past eight or ten years, there has come a waiting and watching season, a careful time of thought and prayer; and now, there is coming forth again to the battle with renewed energy, and zeal, and faith. An acknowledged foe is in our midst. All are agreed upon this. The evil he hath wrought is so palpable, that it is considered by some to be almost a waste of words to dwell upon it. It is no waste of words, though! Fancy and imagination, rhetoric and rhapsody combined can never over-estimate or over-depict the facts of cruelty and grief, sorrow and tears, sickness and deaths that follow in the track of this foe. And the rehearsal of these is the most thrilling and most potent argument to bring the heart and hand together to defeat and to destroy the fearful ravages. Such, however, is not my work this morning.

I want to study, calmly if possible, the method proposed to abolish this evil. But, oh! it is hard to be calm. The eye will see; the ear will hear! Pictures of strangled love, martyred truth, withered sympathies, and blasted joys will appear and reappear before the gaze to distract one's thought to the awfulness of the enemy's deeds. Sad sounds of execration, wailing music echoing from the broken hearts of ill-used wives and the hungry lips of half-fed children, will come surging to one's ears, to prevent one's drifting away into argument and debate while the demon keeps on his accursed way. And yet, I do desire to call your attention, and to keep my own if I can, to an item important indeed to us in every battle and conflict, and which it will be necessary we should settle before we give ourselves and our powers their full sway. I speak especially to the Christian this day, or to him that is prepared to accept Christianity as the truth of God for time and eternity.

I have chosen this text for reasons which will unfold as we proceed. Joshua had just taken command of the children of Israel, and had led them over Jordan into Canaan, and was about to enter upon his first engagement to take a city high and built up with massive walls and gates of heavy iron. While in the neighborhood of this Jericho it is said, "he lifted up his eyes and looked, and, behold, there stood a man over against him with a drawn sword in his hand: and Joshua went unto him, and said, Art thou for us, or our adversaries? And he said, As the captain of the Lord's host am I now come. And Joshua fell on his face to the earth, and did worship, and said, What saith my

Lord unto His servant? And the captain of the Lord's host said unto Joshua, Loose thy shoe from thy foot, for the place where thou standest is holy ground. And Joshua did so." Here God appeared to Joshua to be the captain in the fight. Joshua inquired what the Lord had to say to him. And the Lord said, "Take off your shoes, and remember that I am near."

It is of all importance to us to know if God be on our side, if He be for us or for our adversaries in this great conflict of forces. We may easily suppose, as we often do, that God must be with us, that we are surely right; but here, in this very conflict of our day, our adversaries claim Him, claim His word, claim His nature, and profess a sincerity equal to our own. I want to know, you want to know; I want to feel, you want to feel, this day as you look at the great God we worship and want to obey, standing now with His drawn sword to ride Captain with His host; I say we want to know, "Is He for us, or for our adversaries?"

It is our usual method as Christians to seek for the will of God revealed in His Holy Word. It is this we are called upon to preach in this place. All we say and do must be balanced upon the scales of this revelation of the nature, law, and purpose of the Divine Father. To this Book, therefore, we put the question, "Art thou for us, or for our adversaries?"

Now, it will be necessary to inquire at the outset what is our position, and what is that of our adversaries? If I understand them aright, they claim that the Bible is with them, in that it utters no law or commandment against the use, to a degree at least, of spirituous and intoxicating liquors. And, further, they claim that the uses of temptation are beneficial to the upbuilding of true followers or servants of God, and to the development of true manhood. And, further, that Jesus Christ Himself sanctioned their traffic by His own life and acts when He dwelt on the earth. There may be other minor points dependent upon these three, which our time in one discourse may not permit us to consider.

The position I represent this morning is the precise opposite to each of these, and we shall seek to show our reasons for holding such a place.

In dealing with the first-mentioned claim put forth, it will be our duty to ask, from the standpoint of revealed truth, What is the declared law in the case?

And in view of the wide-reaching interest of the question we have undertaken to discuss, we feel it would be unjust, indeed, to be narrow in the spirit of our investigation. We must come with a large heart and an open mind, free as possible from any prejudice of local or sectional influence.

In seeking for the law which expresses to us the divine will, we must not confound it with the temporary statute or commandment of the circumstantial. In fact, we ought to be able to see that there is wide difference between a law and a commandment. A law is that which is fixed, which exists always, and is founded in the nature of things, which lies behind all written word in statute book or upon table of stone. The law is, "Do this always!" The statute or commandment is, "Do this now." The law can never change, the commandment may, but never in its relation to the law. This is illustrated by the learned scribe coming to Christ and asking, "Which is the greatest commandment in the law?" Mark the answer! "The first is, Thou shalt love the Lord with all thy heart," etc., and the "second is like unto it, Thou shalt love thy neighbor as thyself." Now pay attention to the Scribe's reply. "Thou hast said the truth, for to love the Lord . . . and our neighbor as ourself is more than all burnt-offerings and sacrifices," that is, more than over seventy-five minor statutes that related only to the temporary. And Christ said to that man, "Thou art not far from the kingdom." So the appeal made to Old Testament customs and the early habits of Christian believers, has little bearing upon the proper commandment or statute for to-day. For at no time, either in Syria or Judea, was the habit of intoxication at all prevalent. The contrast between the milk-drinking, cool-blooded shepherds and husbandmen of Palestine in the time of Christ, and the fast-living, nerve-strained people of England and America of to-day, plainly proves that the commandment would not be the same for us. There was not a distillery then, nor an ounce of spirituous liquors in the world. There was not a liquor saloon within a thousand miles of Jerusalem. And even tea, and coffee, and tobacco, and opium, and all the other drugs which it is believed have more or less tendency to foster a craving for stronger stimulants, were entirely unknown there. How is it now? We have, by inheritance, ten generations of these slumbering fires in our blood. There are thousands of saloons in our land whose business it is to kindle and support these appetites.

I know that intoxication in some form is nearly as old as the race. Nearly all people have some kind of an intoxicating beverage; but in Bible days and years intoxication was an exceptional vice, and especially in the countries which are the scenes of Bible history. How very different with us. Here it exists as a stimulus to every other impure and unholy passion, forcing other vices into energy and power; crowding our streets with bloated, reeling caricatures of humanity; building and filling prisons, mad-houses, and gaming hells throughout our land. The only question for us is, What must be the statute in our case? The law remains always the same—the law of love to God and man. The commandment must relate to the law and to the circumstances. If no other people since the days of Adam had a statute to check or obliterate it, that would not make the evil less harmful to us, or the necessity of frustrating it any the less imperative.

The principle of interpretation I have thus employed is general; and is to be applied to all that is local or temporary in Scripture history. The great end of all commandment is that the absolute law may be better revealed and better obeyed.

Again, it is the province of all commandment to protect the general interest. Statutes, though stated in the form of prohibitions, are really *protections*. Though negative in their word, they are positive in their spirit and intent. Instance the Decalogue: "Thou shalt not kill." This is only a beautiful fence put around the gift of life, to *protect* it unto us, that we may have it unmolested. "Thou shalt not commit adultery." This is only a beautiful chain of *protection* thrown about the sacred ties of marriage and of home. "Thou shalt not steal." This is a divine right established to lawfully-acquired property, that we may safely enjoy the harvests of our honest endeavor. "Thou shalt not bear false witness." This is God's shield thrown over our name, when we have striven to keep it pure and clear. . . . And so we could go on to the end, to prove how the whole spirit of the statutes is one of *protection*.

Now this ought to teach us that all laws are absolutely positive. They are courses to pursue, ends to be sought, conditions of welfare, independent of the fact of their utterance or revelation. Elsewhere, the principle has been declared, "Whatsoever a man soweth, that shall he also reap." This is believed; it cannot be otherwise. Every man who sows expects to reap. Every man who sows expects to reap of the kind he sows. Every man expects to reap more than he sows. Any error in the character of the seed is not allowed for to the sower. He reaps according to what he sows; not according to what he intended to sow, or what he thought he had sown. Hence the solemn injunction, "Be not deceived." That is, be not deceived in the seed. Now, here let me ask the question, Have we not been deceived? And are not some of us yet deceived in the nature of the seed we are sowing? There are lingering among us a few who are inclined to believe that what we are calling our great enemy to-day is not necessarily an enemy. I think we all thought so once. I think that for a long time we did look upon it as a friend, which led to our cheer and was a factor in our joy. Let us admit the fact, for our own record declares that at one time all our seasons of gladness sought to be aided and abetted by its presence. But, oh! what a costly experience has been ours? It has been to the nation what it has been to the family; it has been to the family what it has been to the individual—a fraud, a traitor in disguise, a murderer, with a brother's smiling mask.

And now let us look at the reasonable way in which we have been led to find this out. We have been very moderate in our dealings. The wisest of us have said in the past, "Be careful." The moderate, sober advice to the individual has been, "Deal lightly with it, for it is somewhat dangerous." But this advice has been found in the many cases insufficient, on account of the way in which the little has increased the craving for the more. Then, when the individual—our son, brother, friend—has found himself getting enslaved to the habit, he has been exhorted to a stronger exercise of his reason and his inner authority over himself. And finally, when this has not succeeded, the most plausible and moderate adviser has said, "The fault is yours, and if you cannot take it without such evil result, you are one which should prohibit yourself entirely." And, to-day, such is the admitted counsel and reasoning of the most moderate of opinions on this subject. And it is quite in harmony with our present attitude and action. This is the way in which as a people, as a nation, we have thought in the past. We are here to-day as a result of this line of thinking. With us to-day the question is a national one. The moderate nation said first unto its people, you may have a little, but deal lightly with it, for it is an abnormal substance. But the nation found the little increased the appetite of the body corporate to such an extent, that special consideration of the grave question was made, and the nation said, "We must bind ourselves with a stronger commandment; for our growing appetite must be curtailed." But this restrictive statute was found insufficient still. Evils, serious, yea, monstrous, were its burden. And so, now, the most moderate of all counsellors is bound to come forth and say, "If you, as a nation, cannot have it without such evils resulting from its indulgence, you are one that should not have it at all." And the nation, the body corporate, says, "I must abstain."

But, it is replied, "All the members of that body corporate do not say so." Oh, no! Certainly not! Neither did they in the individual body when it was so justly prohibited. A gnawing hunger or thirst down below begged, shouted, demanded a supply. A great conflict ensued in the body, with a cry for "rights" on both sides. "But," you say, "a man ought to have a controlling force somewhere; a true man must or should have self-control." Exactly! but what is self control? There seems to be two selves now in one. It is always a self-control which ever way it goes. But the result depends on which self has the control. The self which controls is the self which is strongest, most developed. We all agree to think we know which self ought to control.

Now, apply this to the body corporate, the nation. We are in that conflict. A nation says, "I must abstain." A nation ought to have self-control as well as a man. Yes, but which is the self that is to control? In the clamor of the members of the body corporate, is the decision to be given to the stomach, the appetite, the flesh, to fulfil, or fill out the lusts thereof; or is that better self of the nation which gives strength, and beauty, and judgment, and purity, and all the positive forms of good, to be the voice of authority, to crush the usurping ones, and to hush their disturbing and discordant clamor? I have heard a few pessimists say that our country has gone so far that it is of no use for its best judgment to issue an edict for its total abstinence; that it is too weak, too far gone to carry it out. Well, if so, what shall we do? Toss it over to stomach rule again, give it a renewed control, and beg by our moral suasion for it to be as easy with us as it possibly can? Oh, no! We will issue the edict. We know our poor body of many members will have some strong yearnings and some awful longings, and much pain; but we will nurse it in our kindest way. We will bring to it the best of nature's healing oils, and soothing anodynes, and helpful tonics; we will quench as fast as possible these feverish thirsts, and pray the patient may soon be freed from all its abnormal yearnings, and find a healthy life again.

But we hasten now to notice the second claim set up by our adversaries to the favor and help of the divine nature and word.

This is a claim that temptation is provided as a method of the Divine to help man to a likeness to Himself and to attain to a perfect manhood. And in connection with this, we have heard it argued that the Divine commands are only to the tempted; and that the tempter is not the subject of rebuke or punishment.

This plea we are prepared to deny *in toto*. As to the last mentioned points, we shall not stay to discuss them. A reader of the Bible will soon perceive the facts. There never was a tempter sent by God to any one. All the tempters ever known, from the first in the garden to the last portrayed in the Apocalypse, have been subject to the curse and the wrath of God.

The commandment against the tempter is as strong everywhere as against the tempted.

There is no better illustration of this than what is recorded in Deuteronomy xiii.

In the face of these facts, it will be well to look more carefully than we have done, perhaps, into this question of the so-called uses or benefits of temptation. I am somewhat prepared to admit that "our adversaries" are not the only ones who hold to this peculiar doctrine. Often, on this point, we are "wounded in the house of our friends." Personally, I am not prepared to admit any uses of temptation, except to the tempter. No man is necessarily any better for being tempted. Nay, I will go further, and leave out the word "necessarily." No man is the better for being tempted. Strength does not come to us from the resisting of temptation specially. Strength comes to us from habit, from persistence on any line, whether tempted or otherwise. The rule is that temptation is a hindrance, and not a help to progress in any direction; and men do not make more rapid progress under temptation than without it, but, rather otherwise. Regular habits beget strength of character independently of temptation. Let a family be brought up to hate evil and to love good, and be kept free to goodness for their earlier years till habits of good are formed, and they are as strong in truth and virtue as those who have struggled, and stumbled, and delayed their course by contact with an evil environment.

Take two boys starting out on any studious pursuit. The one has a quiet home and a quiet locality, and can pursue his studies unmolested. The other lives next door to a lacrosse ground or a base-ball field, and his fondness for such games torments him. Is it a great advantage to have the ball field at hand? By no means. It is urged, as an excuse for him, if he be not equal to his rival, that he had so much to tempt his mind away. Now, I have studied this whole question a good deal, and will preach to you specially upon it some time if you cannot see eye to eye with me now. But, I am convinced that temptation was never any use to any man to develop his character. It is designed always to frustrate a man in his path. Overcoming simply saves from delay or defeat, it does not help progress. And the good Lord knows this. He knows we are in a world where, because we have strayed or because we have yielded, we have lost ground. He does give us grace to conquer, wisdom to escape the tempter, and bids us pray, and after praying, to seek the path where, if possible, no temptation lurks or fowler's snare abides.

Now let us proceed to look at the third claim set forth, which urges that the life and acts of Jesus Christ are consistent with the sale of intoxicants.

What a variety of opinion seems possible on some subjects. I have found as wide a variety on the acts of Jesus relative to this question as on any subject I know. Of course, it is admitted that it depends largely on the seeker what he finds in any locality. You know how different were the reports of the Canaan land brought by Caleb and Joshua, from those brought by the other ten. The land was the same, and was visited at the same season. But the different view was accounted for by the sacred writer in the two being of "another spirit" from the ten. It is much the same in the search of the "spies" that go up to see the testimony of this Book.

As to the character of Christ being one that would have any disposition to lend help to a vice, or an evil of any kind, I think we are fairly agreed. Such He could not do. That He was known to have ever drunk intoxicating liquor, no one can, or will, positively assert. Hence, we have some minds who view Him as one like unto themselves, drinking with publicans and sinners; and other minds see Him moving among them as a new guide and philanthropist, leading them to a higher thought and a higher life. I confess to you I can only see Him in the latter way.

But how about making wine at that Cana wedding? Well, certainly, there has been a variety of interpretations of that act. Probably we have all tried to see in it what we desire to see. I can imagine many an ignorant temperance fanatic wishing that record could only have been erased from the sacred page. I can imagine that he would skip it when it came in order for the reading at family worship. It is the only thing he has against the Divine Lord. Well, I must say, I have never felt so. You may account for it as you may; but it has never read to me, even in my unprejudiced boyhood, as if Jesus made any wine, in the ordinary sense at all. If I had read it as others and believed, therefore, as they do, I should be disposed from the analogy of faith to believe it to be not that kind which the wise man had forbidden others to "look upon," or at which to "tarry long." But, as I say, I have never had to believe that He made any. When I found that many others, wiser and abler in exegesis, and in interpretation than I, had different views from mine, I did honestly yield my simple reading of it to their view; but I could not read their ideas into it, and so I just read it as I could. I have never undertaken to press my view upon others. In nearly three years' ministry you have never heard it; but though I have not been dogmatic on it, I aver to you I cannot read it as others do. Look at the narrative as I view it. It will be no more unreasonable than to read it in the light of other minds He was at the feast. The wine-drinkers were partaking. He seems to have been aside. They come to Him through His mother. She says, "They have no wine." She knew not what He would do, knew not what He could do. And, now, what said He? "Fill the water-pots with water." Mark that! "Water-pots and water;" why not "bring hither the wine bottles?" Why did He discard the wine bottles? "Fill the water-pots with water. And they filled them up to the brim." Now, "pour it out to them." Give them that to drink! And they did. And such was the difference—not the sameness mind you—such was the difference that they said it was better than anything they had tasted at the feast. The lesson to me always was: Water-pots and water with the blessing of Christ upon it made to have an exhilarating influence before all wine. Would Christ have them, and have us, learn that lesson? Was His action there designed to teach it? It always seems so to me. Now, I say I am not dogmatic. I don't say that is the only real, genuine meaning of that act. But I do say that the letter killeth, and the spirit of the thing seems to present no other lesson so sublime to me. I have weighed the evidence in favor of other interpretations with this result: If He wanted to make wine and show His sympathy with the usage; if He saw no danger in the custom of the day, and wished to add His force to it for all time to come, it would seem as if He took a very unusual course —I mean for Him—of doing so. He honored the bread and the fishes when they fell short of a sufficiency by using the little at hand. But He seemed to repudiate the wine bottles, which must have had some dregs which He could have multiplied. His Father, through the ancient prophet, had honored the barrel of meal and the cruse of oil, by using the power of increase upon the material needed. But not so here. I aver to you, this is to me very significant. Moreover, there is a peculiarity about the emphasis always placed upon the water in the reference to this miracle. The most insignificant reference to it says, "Where Jesus made the water wine." Why not say simply, Where Jesus made the wine?

And now, for one moment let us hypothesize. Suppose we should be correct in thinking that Jesus did desire to place the water in its own rightful place at the head of all beverages. Suppose He did see the danger that should come to mankind by the festive wine cup, and its associations; and suppose He did desire to leave a lesson on record such as a sober age two thousand years after should be able to read with profound appreciation of His foresight and provision. I say, suppose that. Then was not His whole method of action most beautifully consistent with such a purpose? For, verily, though the world has had its wine in the early part of its feast, and Christ has come to dwell forever on the earth by His spirit, do we not see that He is discarding everywhere the wine bottles, and filling up the water-pots; and as the purer world lifts up its glass of water, so long displaced by the poisonous drugs, to its thirsty lips, it shall exultantly exclaim, "The best of the wine at the last of the feast." Oh, ye whose festivities ye would keep bright and clear to the last hour: "Fill the water-pots with water, and bear it to the governor of the feast." So just let me say, then, that there is no warrant in Christ's action at Cana of Galilee to lead me to place Him in accord with the wine drinking customs of any age. I wish to repeat, however, that I should find no great difficulty in accepting the view held by many others, that He provided for them the customary juice of the grape. I should not perceive any great incongruity in such an act, especially in a country where no spirituous liquors could be found and intoxication was but little known, and where in the company there was no predisposition toward it. I should perceive His sympathy for them in their hour of need, stooping to habits and customs indulged in by them with the purest and most innocent intent.

But my time has gone. I have only glanced, after all, at the inconsistency of the argument for strong drink being sustained by the Bible. From beginning to end, its revelation is one of a divine purpose and a divine effort to free man from every error, and every evil; to rid this sorrowing earth of all its tears, and sighs, and groans. At all times it has chosen to speak to man as he required. It has dictated first as to self-preservation and purity, then to the brother's care. Its method has always been to reveal a law, then enact a commandment, then persuade by the varied motives of reward and punishment to that end. As workers, we labor with the Bible to reach its coveted destination. We have embraced its law as that which shall be unto our mouth as "better than thousands of gold and silver." Where there is doubt about the commandment or doctrine, we shall strive "to do His will," His general will—and we shall then "know of the doctrine whether it be of God." And we shall obey the divine injunction of prayer, "If any man lack wisdom, let him ask of God, who giveth to all men liberally and upbraideth not."

We are exhorted to moral suasion. We have used it long and well. We will use it still. But it falls with weak effect on the very ones who praise it as the only successful and legitimate way. We may gather the distiller, and brewer, and bar-tender together, and bid them see the moral ruin they have made in the space of only one passing year. We may show them the deep dyes with which they have colored the picture of human sorrows, and the dense black shade in which they have filled the background; and one would almost think they would cease their traffic, go their way, and sin no more. But is it so? Nay! We may show them the footprints of their bygone track, and see how closely on the verge of hell they run; we may walk them for an hour among the graves—the little graves—the graves of the helpless, innocent, who, but for them might have been prattling and smiling now; graves which the spirit fiend has dug and filled. We could lift before them the coffin lid where the young mother lies stark and livid, with her dead baby on her breast, and the red dark mark upon her bosom, not yet rubbed off by even the cold hand of death, the cruel legacy which a drunken husband gave her to carry to the tomb, and to bear witness against him at the bar of God, which her reluctant lips refuse to speak. And, I confess, when they see all this, one would expect to see them fall down upon their knees among those lonely graves, and by the outraged ashes of the sleepers there vow to that God who reads the secrets of the human heart, that never again should the fiery goblet be passed from their hands to do its cruel work of death. But does it accomplish its work with these? You know too well the answer. Yet we will continue to labor with both hands. The law is against it; the everlasting law of brotherly love. The commandment is not. It must be made harmonious with the law. We seek that end to-day. Oh, cannot we all be united in this cause? Our cause is one which can never injure truth, or purity, or love. There is no divine or human reason why this sublime end and aim of a sober nation should not be a charm to us all and a bond to link us eternally to one another and to God. We are called upon to express our desire that a statute shall be enacted in harmony with the eternal law of purity and mutual helpfulness. Let us speak plainly, and pray God to speed the day when no liquor shall be provided for our growing generation; but we shall obey the divine and fatherly injunction, "Make no provision for the flesh to fulfil the lusts thereof."

IX.

PERFECT.

"Be ye therefore perfect, even as your Father which is in heaven is perfect."

MATTHEW v. 48.

PERFECT.

I FEEL a keen and immortal responsibility in preaching to you as a people. Some of you have a wonderful experience behind you. I hear you so often tell of the great times of refreshing through which you have passed. I hear you quote the names of the honored men and mighty in the Scriptures at whose feet you have sat as disciples year in and year out for many seasons. You have had, as your record tells, great privileges; and they have been unto you great blessings or great curses. You are much richer or much poorer than other people, by just so much as your higher privileges have been improved or otherwise. I came among you feeling that I must seek, more than ever I had done, to know the larger will of God for myself, and then for you; and it has been my pleasure to study it and strive to unfold it to your gaze. And I do not hesitate to say that there has been both exaltation and humiliation associated with the task. Viewing with the eye of earnest faith the land of promise that lies before us, and hearing the gracious callings of the Spirit and the Word of God, the heart joyed with hope of such attainment. But when the feet have clung too tightly to present ground, and weights have been discovered that we never felt till we tried to rise ; and our attention has been called from the beautiful prospect to the entangled self, the humiliation has displaced the former joy. It always does. It is precious to study, to gaze upon the exceeding riches of the grace of God toward us; it is painful, then, in the light of these to measure the true relation of ourselves to them. And so, oh, how often, I have loathed myself in my uneven way. How at times I have hated my own soul for its narrowness of love! How I have sometimes almost shrunk from my pulpit because I felt I would rather not have to deal with any other soul but my own for the while ! How I have felt as if I ought to go away for my spiritual health, as some do for their physical health ! But I have toiled on, labored on ; and I have thought of you as I have of myself. I have credited you with the same convictions. I have brought out my thought for your study as well as my own. I have not hidden from you the deepest intents of my heart. I have told you I was seeking upward, desiring the higher, the truer, the better. And if there is a better, wiser, higher life for me, there is for you, for all. I long for the world to see the beauty and glory of Christ in us; and oh, I am sore tempted and tried over the poor exhibit we make before that world, of the infinite pity and love. And so you have noticed I am sure that some days I have come to you speaking cheerily, in hope; and other days, perhaps, despondingly, in despair. I have been in both atmospheres of thought and feeling as regards the position, attitude and work of the Church of Christ in the world. There are few to cheer me when I am sad; and my most of sadness comes from brooding over the Saviour's testimony, "The harvest truly is great, but the laborers are few;" and His sorrowful view of the sinners' rejection, "Ye will not come unto Me that ye might have life."

It is somewhat in this sadness I labor to-day. I am not as bright as I am sometimes, for the shadow of a sinning and dying world has fallen on my brow, and the cruel carelessness of my past about it, I have not been able to overcome. But I have turned my face toward the rising sun and asked from the hills their help, and I pursue my way along to meet the difficulty, and by faith in Him who is the final conqueror, I want to qualify for the fray and the victory. And I believe there are many hearts here with me to-day. And what must be the line of our thoughts! Oh, you will say, take the best you can get, the sublimest you can hold before us as a possible destiny. And so I ask you to study with me the Saviour's wonderful command, or exhortation, or promise, or whatever you may choose to call this text, "Be ye therefore perfect, even as your Father which is in heaven is perfect."

It seems to me that this subject is in the spirit of the age in which we live. In the past, there has always seemed to be a theoretical belief in salvation from sin, but a practical belief, that we must all, to some small extent at least, indulge, to retain our human place. Practically our commandments read, "Thou shalt not kill" much; "Thou shalt not steal" much; "Thou shalt not commit adultery" much. But it is evident now that in the thought of the best philanthropists, total abstinence is coming to be the only practical solution of the problems of evil. Its possibility is proven by many witnesses, and all are beginning to plead for its public and private enforcement. This is so in the narrower realm of "temperance" activity; it is so likewise in the wider realm of "all evil." The blessed book we take as our monitor encourages us to live for and obtain a perfect deliverance from sin; and the gracious utterance of the Saviour who gave Himself for us is found in the text, "Be ye perfect, even as your Father which is in heaven is perfect."

I have no purpose to enter into any theological disquisition this morning. I dislike this thing as much as you do. I have never wanted to argue over those things which the blessed Saviour tells us can only be proven by experience. I believe now, however I may have thought in years of less information, in perfection of being. And I want you to believe in it too. I do not want you to cut down your ideas or conceptions of the possibilities of the human being in the salvation inherited in Jesus Christ. He has distinctly declared His mission to be our "access to the Father." To as many as receive Him, He giveth "power to become the sons of God." In this inheritance let no one come along with limitations. We scorn them. We have our relations with the Infinite. The text says, "Your Father." That satisfies me. I would not have believed perfection possible but for that. Now, I have the perpetual witness that I am a child of God. And with this upon me, you may remind me as you choose of my limitations, of my youth, of my inexperience; I can yet look up, as can any child, and claim the largeness of my Father's life for myself.

Indeed, in the very nature God gave us it is hard to find a finitude. No one yet has shown a limit to human capacity, or successfully said, "Thus far shalt thou go and no farther." How much man can know, or how much man can do, are questions no wise one would attempt to answer. Science fixes no limit for the human mind to reach in its acquisition of knowledge. Art has not dampened human genius by saying, there is no better than this possible. Wealth has not stopped even at a millionaire to beckon its seekers onward; and, if it had, man's very reach after the beyond would impel him to vault every barrier raised, and pursue his way to a larger achievement.

Verily, then, no other counsel would bring satisfaction to the sublime nature God hath given us, than to be perfect as anything we can behold anywhere. Our beholdings can never be beyond our possible achievements. For my own part, it has always been the dream of my own outward looking to behold, in the unfolding will of the Father, a perfection of being for man, not yet ever seen in creatures upon which our backward gaze of history has looked. A brighter day, when the sursoundings of sin shall pass away under the law of the regeneration of love, shall reveal to us the perfect outcome of the will of God for man. The past has been too full of opposition to the will of God to show us any perfect ideal. The good man has been bruised, grieved, crucified in every age. This is not really an essential part of the heritage of a child of God. There is no purpose so plain than that God would save His loved ones eventually the pain of one angry word. But while we pass through the tide of selfishness, and ignorance, and sin which surrounds us, we must seek to know the best attitude of mind and heart to assume, that the ills may be rebuked and overcome. And these are taught us in our Saviour's spirit. And all our studies of His exemplified graces should only help us to keep in view the perfect destiny of man; and place ourselves as heroes in the field, willing to endure the cross and the transient shame, that we may help to bring forward the heritage which belongs to a victory over sin and error. It is in order to bring to man this destiny of peace and goodness combined, that we, the earlier disciples, must accept the condition: "In the world ye shall have tribulation, but in Me ye shall have peace." Our joy must be like our Master's, "set before us," and must be so strong that it will enable us to "endure the cross, despising the shame."

Perfection, then, for us will be to fill up perfectly the measure of our fidelity to the end to which we are called in Christ. If ours is the day of battle, if the glory to be won for humanity is not yet achieved, we must be perfect soldiers upon the field. Our imperfection, as such, will surely cause delay in the coming of the Son of man in His glory. Here comes the necessity of having the spirit of Christ in us. If the Christ-idea is to be the redeeming force in this world of sin and error, we must carry that idea along in its truth. Can a worldly life save the world to love and brotherhood? Can a life unto self alone ever draw all men away from selfishness and its sin? Oh! never. Such is really a godless life. I know we do not think so, but we are wrong in our estimate of God. Perhaps we have not been properly taught. If Paul, or Peter, or John were with us daily, preaching in our churches and living on our streets, we would, perhaps, have better ideas of God and His will concerning us.

I hold myself, as the preacher, the guilty one before you. It may be I have not so fulfilled the law of Christ before you. We have been overcome by the world's thought and spirit, it may be. We may not have preached a full enough Gospel. Well, brethren, accept the confession, and hear the truest Gospel. I have striven, in the spell of a deepening attachment, to place before you the life and spirit of our blessed Lord, the pattern of our lives; nay, more, the inspiration, the indwelling source of our new industry and our new being, the best way I know how. And, if the "grace of our Lord Jesus Christ," of which we spoke a few days ago, has at all touched us; if our long blinded eyes have been unsealed to behold a true glory beaming forth in the generous and lowly service rendered for us in the humiliation and the cross; if, at all, the spirit of that Saviour has touched us into life, and breathed the temper of heaven into our earthly flesh, we will not ask whether His life, or our own, is most like our Father's, or which is the nobler and more royal for a man. I have been impressed with the beautiful way in which Dr. Dykes sets out the truth of the divine in life. He helped me to see how Jesus Christ gave us new views of what divineness really is. We had been so accustomed to conceive that God's greatness and glory lay most of all in His supremacy, in the fact that He was "Lord and Master" of every creature, that for His honor were all things made, that He could, when He desired, command a universe of menials, and that all creation spake or sang His glorious praise. And like the Gentiles with their kings, we called Him "greatest" because He exercised an authority over us. But Jesus Christ came to teach us better things than these, and as we know them, they will put us into a different attitude.

When the King's Son came among us, we did well to

call Him "Master and Lord," for so He was. But He was all the while as one who served us. And He taught us that He never spoke a word or did a deed that was not given Him of His Father. And so He would have us learn that the very divinest part of God's relationship to all His creatures lies here; that, being Lord of all, He makes Himself the servant of all. Doth not "day unto day" bespeak Him our provider, attendant, benefactor? and "night unto night" show Him as creation's unwearied watcher? "The lions roar and He feedeth them. Not a sparrow falls but He heeds it. The lilies spin not, yet He clothes them. The patient minister to each creature's need, in whose loving eyes nothing is too minute to be remembered, nor too mean to be served; He is forever, with tender, humble carefulness, laying His might, and His providence, and His inventiveness, and His tastefulness at the service of all creation." And in this is declared the true "Glory of God;" for what is His glory if it be not in His love? There is verily nothing greater. So is the universe the mirror of its Creator's glory, by so much as it shows unto us how lavish He is of His love, how He restricts not care upon the smallest, how He condescends to adorn the meanest, and how He is supremely glad when His creatures are glad. " Jesus, the only begotten Son, hath declared Him." When and where? When He spake, "I came not to be ministered unto, but to minister"; and where He washed His disciples' feet and bid them, "As I have loved you, that ye should also love another."

If, then, the "throne of glory," upon which the God Father of all is seated, be a throne of love and ministration; from the standpoint of such a throne, look out upon a world of sin. Look out upon a world with ideas of God so vague and so erratic; a world who thought God as one of themselves; a world whose ideas all lay in the narrowest forms of selfdom. And mark, then, how needful that some one should come and show us the Father ere we could ever have any fellowship with Him or be brought up from our ugliness to His beauty. And perceive how—even in the wisdom of God—such was not possible, save in the way we have lately unfolded; that He should come down to our conditions, and live in our contracted circumstances, and give up independence for dependence, riches for poverty, joy for sorrow, life for death, and be "made sin for us, who knew no sin, that we might be made the righteousness of God through Him." And when He had gathered about Him a few who beheld His glory and longed to share it, He committed unto them the word and work of this reconciliation for humanity.

Remember how He said they "could not see" the work, the duty, the needs, or the glory of the kingdom, unless they were "born of His spirit." Oh, it is easy to understand that now. Verily, how could they? None but such a spirit could see such a path or such a destiny! And then remember how He left them alone and went away, and sent His spirit to fill them and to fit them for the sublime work which He undertook on our behalf. And remember how His followers did see the nature and extent of the work which lay before them, and how they did always feel the need of a present Christ-spirit to aid them in the toil. And remember how they did not for one moment count their lives dear unto themselves, so that they might finish their course with joy, and the message they had received of the Lord Jesus to testify the gospel of the grace of God. Hear how they received the sufferings that their lot among sinful men brought upon them: "Who now rejoice in my sufferings for you, and fill up that which is behind of the affliction of Christ in my flesh for his body's sake, which is the Church."

"The Holy Ghost;" "The Grace of our Lord Jesus Christ;" "The Father of Mercies;" they are all one! It means the same thing, whether it is said, "Receive ye the Holy Ghost," or "Let this mind be in you which was also in Christ Jesus," or "Be ye perfect, even as your Father which is in heaven is perfect." They are all of love. The glory of the Father is that "God is love." The glory of the Son is "the love of Christ which passeth knowledge." The glory of the Spirit is, "the fruit of the Spirit is love." "Love is of God, and he that dwelleth in love, dwelleth in God and God in Him."

It is this love of God for all His creatures, this love that "lays down its life for us," which gives eternal and immovable emphasis to that "ought" which says "We ought to lay down our lives for the brethren." And it is this fellowship with Christ in love, I set before you to-day. It is the Saviour who saves, who says, "Be perfect as your Father." If God is our Father, if we are conceived and born of Him, we can, we shall, we *must* be perfect after His kind. Had a teacher come to us saying, "Be perfect as God, the One only, true, wise, immortal and invisible," we would have staggered at the command and called the teacher mad. But when He comes revealing to us a fatherhood in God, and declaring to us the generating power of an incoming and indwelling spirit, we can see that He is not mad, but "speaks forth the words of truth and soberness." Our hearts bound with joy at the very command, knowing that He who spake it "knoweth the Father," and "knoweth our frame and remembereth that we are dust." Oh! what a heritage! what a birthright! May not one of us be so eternally foolish as to sell it for a mess of earth's temporary pottage.

Are you eager to-day for your promised inheritance in God? Does it stand out before you as the most desirable of all good? Then are you "not far from the kingdom?" You will obediently sell all you have and give to the poor, that you may have treasure in heavenly things.

To those who are already won by this love of Christ, and who pant to be the possessors and distributors of it to the needy hearts of mankind, it can easily come. You need little teaching now to reach it. Simply give up all your heart to receive it. It is God's delight to give it to every one that asketh. He only needs an empty heart to fill. Bring your pitcher to the fountain to-day and you shall go away refreshed yourself, and "the water which He shall give you shall be in you a well of water springing up into everlasting life."

This is what we need to help us to win souls. The seekers after purity, peace, repose, forgiveness, love, good of any kind, will come to us to help them, if they see us loving toward one another and toward the lost.

It is imperfect love which brings imperfect service; and imperfect service brings imperfect results. Do we believe these things? Then we can never go back from them uncondemned. We can never unsee. We can not ever unknow. "If we know these things, happy are we if we do them."

There are pressing needs upon us to-day. We are disposed to push the burdens away from us and let others take them and bear them. We shrink from the cross of our Lord, and claim the easy places for our coward souls. We "kick against the pricks," like Saul of old, and only goad ourselves into irritation and madness. Stop! Lord, turn on the light and show us two things! Show us our real state! Coward, selfish, shirking, worldly, having at times the form of godliness, but not proving the power of it. Lord God forgive us, we are ashamed. Is there aught for us better? What shall we be? What shall we do? Show us the needed thing; the cross to take, the work to begin. We will trust Thee for the peace and glory to follow.

Shall this be our prayer, and our attitude of soul to-day? Verily let it be so now. We lay our souls at His feet. We give up our all to Him. If our lives are not better, more sweet, more powerful, adorning the doctrine of God our Saviour, then convince us of sin, point the finger of scorn at us, call us hypocrites, hoot at us as defamers of the character of God. Say of us, "Pretty children, these, of a Father who dies for men."

Father, we come home to-day. We have been dominated by the world, and led away. But we feel that our Father's house and our Father's heart is the place for us. We are cold. The storm has beat upon us without. Warm us in Thine embrace. Thou art truly our father; let us truly be Thy children. Let Thy love possess and fill us, control and direct us, now, at all times, in all moments. Thy promises cheer us, let Thy Spirit empower us. And then, let the world feel the impulse of our love as brethren born of God. Amen!

X.

THE PULPIT AND SOCIAL QUESTIONS.

"*The Spirit of the Lord God is upon me; because the Lord hath anointed me to preach good tidings unto the meek; He hath sent me to bind up the brokenhearted, to proclaim liberty to the captives, and the opening of the prison to them that are bound; to proclaim the acceptable year of the Lord, and the day of vengeance of our God; to comfort all that mourn; to appoint unto them that mourn in Zion, to give unto them beauty for ashes, the oil of joy for mourning, the garment of praise for the spirit of heaviness.*"

ISAIAH lxi. 1-3.

THE PULPIT AND SOCIAL QUESTIONS.

SO spake the tender-hearted and devoted Isaiah to his people in the hour of the conflicts. And so spake the Christ, the Son of Man, when He sat in the synagogue of Nazareth and read these words from Esaias, and declared, "This day is this Scripture fulfilled in your ears." The voice of the prophet, the voice of the Christ, the voice of the evangelist or teacher in the name of Christ is a voice of help for the needy, of relief for the oppressed, of liberty for the bound, of life for the dead. If the pulpit cannot bring help for human needs, it can have no inspiration to keep it alive, and it can have no welcome to keep it engaged. When it fulfils the mission declared in the text, it finds abundant inspiration, for the "Spirit of the Lord is upon" the preacher; and it finds a liberal welcome, for the needy ones abound; and they have well learned that the pulpit speaks more kind words to more needy hearts than all the voices of earth. I am to speak to you to-night upon the sphere of the pulpit, and especially as it relates to the great social questions which affect all human life.

To occupy a pulpit by legitimate authority is one of the highest honors a man can sustain. In comparison with his position at the time he stands there, that of the senator in the hall of assembly, or even that of the monarch on the throne of the realm, is insignificant; for the pulpit occupant is an ambassador of Jesus Christ, the only Saviour of human destiny, sent to deal with men on questions which involve their very highest interests in the life that now is, as well as in that which is to come. And of all public stations, the pulpit is unquestionably the most responsible. No man should enter it without the most serious consideration; and whether he comes from the shades of a learned university, or from the workshop of the mechanic, or from the labors of the field, he should tread the ground with solemn step, and strive to fulfil the task before him as under the immediate eye of heaven.

The pulpit is not a common platform, upon which any man may spring at any hour, under any impulse, and air his opinions upon any subject of dispute. The pulpit claims an authority to speak, because it claims an authority of knowledge. It speaks the words of

Him who said, "I am the Truth." The man who enters it, then, must confine his utterances to that which has the authoritative preface, "Thus saith the Lord." But while this may, at first sight, indicate that the sphere of the pulpit is narrow, and that bounds are put upon the utterances that are to be made there; yet, upon a little reflection, it will be seen that the opposite of this is the truth. The pulpit has the broadest scope, because it deals with the universal good of men. There is nothing in earth that is worthy the occupation of God-given time, and God-given talent, and God-given strength, but is worthy the attention of the pulpit and worthy of its Christly counsels. The theme of the pulpit is Redemption. It is called a Gospel. It is called the "word of life." It is announced as a message of peace and good-will through love.

Wherever is strife, wherever is discord, wherever is disagreement, wherever is friction among men, there is a place where the Gospel is needed, and there is a place where the Gospel can heal, if it be received and followed as the counsels of God. If I may be allowed a personal reference, let me say that I feel more and more every day that the time is at hand when the true servant of Jesus Christ should be, not less an orator, perhaps, but more a teacher and friend of human kind, a being more like Christ Himself. It might lead to his crucifixion to follow the Master closely, and speak the truth fearlessly, but he is unworthy the call who is not willing to endure the cross. I feel that, as a class of public leaders, we have never realized as we should the greatness of our empire in thought, and love, and action. I feel certain we have not filled up the measure of Christ's example before us.

When slaves tilled the ground all about the country church, and the lash of the slave-whip could be heard above the psalm of the worshippers, the pulpit was forbidden by the popular voice to preach on the rights of man. When brewers, and distillers, and saloon keepers, and liquor vendors held high seats in society and Church, the pulpit was charged not to speak on temperance. And too often and too long was the pulpit coward enough to hold its peace at the beck of the strong ones in evil pursuits. And in a great many other branches of human life and conduct has the public voice sought to shape the utterance of the pulpit to suit its ways, and thus to compress into half its size and half its power this medium of divine communication to the children in need. But these things are changing. Truth is beginning, upon every hand, to assert its right in God to be heard and to be obeyed. And it will be seen more and more that the pulpit is really the guardian of all man's dearest interests, and must, like its founder, Jesus, not only speak faith, and righteousness, and future life, but it must have compassion on the multitude, and ask, "Where shall this people get bread?" "Christianity, you will all agree, is a universal or all-sided good, and its genius throughout is love. And now, as the love of a mother stands ready to defend her child against any manner of foe, be it disease or a robber, cold, heat or rain, bad company or savage brute, so Christianity must not stop to ask what particular kind of a grief is falling upon humanity, but must wait only long enough to know there is a trouble, and must seek until it find the needed alleviation."

If, then, there is any grievance in the family of earth's children, by which they hinder rather than help one another, it is the true spirit of the pulpit to place itself and all its resources at the feet of humanity for their relief. If the occupant of the pulpit has no message that he feels is related to their difficulty, it must be because he does not know his lesson well. Then should he "study to show himself a workman approved of God and that needeth not to be ashamed, rightly dividing the word of truth, that each may receive a portion of meat in due season." The Gospel of Christ possesses within its composition the means of allaying all enmity and all destructive elements in society, and the means of infusing love and life and all the constructive forces by which the peace of earth is to be ushered in, and brotherhood is to be built up and maintained in the beauty of the Father's will.

It will be in harmony with our present purpose to mark, first, how far Christ Himself lent His voice as a preacher to the earthly affairs of men. Oh, how we wish that humanity would only study Christ more in all their pursuits! It would be a marvel to many of them, we are sure, to see how they have removed Christ from the sphere in which He placed Himself for human good. His Gospel was a Gospel for earth! First and foremost a Gospel for earth! What has been the record of man's loss? The history of the original loss of man, as given by divine revelation, is the loss of his garden; or, in other words, of his earth. And any one who will look with earnest and honest heart into the history of God's people, and of His dealings with them, will find that God connected at all times temporal prosperity with the knowledge and keeping of His will and word. God knew very well that a Gospel that would not save on earth would have a poor recommendation for saving anywhere else. The counsels of God, through all His prophets, bore directly upon this form of good. David strung his harp to sing this song; Isaiah's lute was filled with this melody; Jeremiah's lyre accompanied his songs of weeping over gates broken down and gardens overgrown with weeds; Ezekiel's clarion aroused with the warning and the promise, couched always in the terms of earthly weal or woe. And so also did the final teacher preach and teach for the welfare of man, and his comfort and happiness upon the earth. The disciples were to work and pray for that. When He sent them forth He bade them do for men any necessary thing which men could not do for themselves. He said, "Heal the sick," for the Gospel comes to dispel disease. He said, "Comfort those that mourn;" He said, "Cast out devils," make homes glad, make hearts glad, do anything that will give truth, and health, and life, and peace to man! If Christ had anything to say about heaven, it was for the time when earth's work was done. But how strange that men have been so long reversing the divine order! Again, we say, if Christ's Gospel would not be a salvation for earth, it would not be for heaven. Men need it on earth. Here is the sorrow requiring relief; there is none there! Here is the darkness to be illuminated; there is none there! Here is the labor that tires, and here are the conflicting interests that wear us down; there are none there! Here is the sin, here is the error, here is the loss, here is the struggle, here is the defeat!

Oh! then, here is the place for the good to be done, and here is the kind of good that needs the doing! And Jesus saw it. He "saw the multitudes and was moved with compassion, because they were as sheep having no shepherd." "He beheld the city and wept over it." He turned with pity upon a crowd of hungry faces, and said, "Whence shall we buy bread that these may eat?" In the synagogue at Galilee He appropriated to Himself the language of Esaias, "The Spirit of the Lord God is upon me, because the Lord hath appointed me to preach good tidings to the meek;" and on the brow of the honored mountain He declared as the good tidings, "Blessed are the meek, for they shall inherit the earth."

It would not be like the wise Saviour to leave the most desirable things out of a prayer He was teaching His own disciples, especially one which He saw would live two thousand years and move the tongue of infants and of fathers with the tenderest emotion still. And yet there is not one word in the Lord's Prayer about fitting us for heaven, or about our going to heaven; but earnest and plain words about heaven coming to us, of earth being made like heaven, *i.e.*, about the laws of heaven—the laws of life, and love, and brotherhood, that made heaven—coming to reign and rule here to the same glorious end. I believe that the reason so many of the children of earth are careless about the Gospel of Christ, is because it has been preached so long as a Gospel, not for this world or its active and interesting life, but for a distant world of which we know but very little, and which must be, therefore, of lesser interest to most of us. I am inclined to believe that the faith of the pulpit lost its hold over the past century. It got discouraged, and ceased to expect the Gospel to correct and to harmonize things here; and so, placed all its emphasis on a preparation for a future life by a seclusion or retirement from this one. Pity, indeed, that such an error should ever have captivated the teaching of the Church. If this Gospel that is preached to mankind in the vigor and buoyancy of youth be only a Gospel for another life when this one is over; I am sure I do not wonder that so many put it off till that time is drawing nigh, deeming that it will be time enough for that when it comes; as says the Master, "Take no thought for the morrow, for the morrow shall take thought for the things of itself. Sufficient unto the day is the evil thereof."

Then, let me just ask your attention for a few moments to the great sermon by the Saviour Himself, when He was establishing His kingdom on earth, laying down its principles and showing its ends. He opens His discourse by naming and blessing all those members of human society that are needy and feel their needs, and those who are doing all they can to alleviate one another's ills of life. "The poor in spirit"—those who in the long conflict of opposing forces are depressed and sad; to those He says, The kingdom is coming to cheer and to lift you up. "They that mourn"—to these He says, as by the wording of our text, "The Lord hath appointed me to comfort all that mourn." "The meek"—blessed are ye! for, "the earth," which ye, sitting quietly still, have seen go out of your hands into the hands of the proud and haughty, "the earth shall be your inheritance." Those who long for the right, "hunger and thirst after righteousness," sigh after the good, "ye shall be filled with it" and be satisfied. "The merciful"—ye that have forgiven the wrongs of men against you and have not sought revenge—ye shall see mercy obtain in the earth as the result of your exercise and seed sowing. "The pure in the heart"—to your unbleared and single eye God shall appear, and you shall see Him, and be able to follow Him. "The peace makers"—ye that have stood in the hot places, between the striving brothers, and sought for peace and good-will; the world shall yet see you and call you the offspring of God. "The persecuted for righteousness' sake"—ye that have stood for the right amid the jeers and scoffs, and taunts, and blows of the strikers, and of the sons of vengeance, and the children of wrath; "blessed are ye," for ye have fought for and won the reign of the good; "yours is the kingdom of heaven." Now let us remember that all this promise about the "kingdom of heaven" means "on earth," as is intimated in the Saviour's words of prayer which He gave His followers.

And now, in this wonderful inaugural sermon, there follows the Saviour's method of filling the earth with all this promised goodness and brotherhood. To these good ones He says, "Ye are the salt of the earth," ye shall season it if ye lose not the seasoning power; and "ye are the lights of the world," ye are as "a city set on a hill which cannot be hid." Do not think, said He, that all the law of right which you have heard from Moses and the prophets, and which you have been striving to keep, is to fail or be done away. Do not think that all your struggles are in vain. I have come to see it completely carried into effect. Did the prophets say, "As I live, saith the Lord, all the earth shall be filled with the glory of God?" I came to see it done! Did the prophets say, "Nation shall not lift up sword against nation, neither shall they learn war any more?" I came to see it done! Did they say, "The wilderness, and the barren and uncultivated parts shall be glad for the new life, and the desert shall rejoice and blossom as the rose?" I came to see it done! Did the law say to mankind, "Thou shalt not kill?" Did it say, "Thou shalt not commit adultery?" Did it say, "Thou shalt not steal?" Did it say, "Thou shalt not bear false witness?" Did it say, "Thou shalt love thy neighbor as thyself?" "Verily, I say unto you, till heaven and earth pass, not one jot or tittle of the law shall fail till all be fulfilled." "I came not to destroy the law, but to fulfil." I came to see it done!

And following this emphatic and inspiring declaration, He lays down the laws of His kingdom. These are no special change from the old laws, only a little more explicit rendering of them, becoming to the additional light and experience of the people since they were first given. And following the utterance of these revised statutes, we have plainly announced the relation which this kingdom shall sustain to the existing world, and to the errors and evil forces that actuate its troublous career. Mark its relation to enemies, and the law of forgiveness and forbearance. Mark its relation to hoarding earthly treasures, and keeping them thereby out of their spheres of designed usefulness and fruit; how that by hoarding we do not provide so well for the morrow as by resowing. That which is hoarded the moth may corrupt or the thief steal; but that which is put to service, or cast into surrounding forces, as the seed, shall reproduce, and make the morrow the richer thereby. Mark the relation of His words to one another's character and life; how we are to judge others as we would have others judge us—a more likely way of coming to the truth than the usual way. "Therefore," says He, "as ye would that men should do to you, do ye even so to them," and this will fulfil "the law and the prophets;" this will see the thing done!

And then follows a very practical exhortation based upon this "golden rule." The connection between them is too often lost by the careless reader. "Enter ye in at the strait gate." What strait gate? The one just set up—the golden rule. Christ had just narrowed down all our acts to the strait confines, "as ye would that men should do to you." He says this gate leads to "life," to human life, in its love, in its fruitfulness of good, in its brotherhood, in all that the life of humanity ought to be. This is the constructive way, the way that builds up. It is the way of the law, the way of the prophets, the way of the Son of Man, the way that "leadeth unto life." The "broad way" is the opposite way; where men have no regard as to how they would like to be treated, the "go-as-you-please" way, the "do-as-you-want-to" way, with no guards, no restraints; where passion can play, and lust can demand its desire, and whim can flippantly crack its whip at

15

will. This way "leads unto destruction." It is destructive, pulling down, disintegrating in its whole essential method and spirit. Society cannot live by this law, or rather, license. This is the "broad road" that leadeth unto death. "And many there be that go in thereat, because strait," confining, restricting, correcting "is the way that leadeth unto life, and few there be that find it." Doubtless, it is harder to find the narrow way. And in the Saviour's day there were few, indeed, that found it. But He came to be that way, to live it before men, to show men how, by living it, and others following Him, a great constructive living power would take hold upon humanity; and then many there would be who would find it. The broad road had been the way along which, like sheep without a shepherd, the multitude had run; but now the "Good Shepherd" who is also the "Door," or strait gate, would lead the many into the way of eternal life. When, on the side of Golgotha hill, that gate was swung wide open upon its hinges, but three women and one man stood by to watch the open portal ready to enter in. Now, in every nation, of every tongue, where the strait gate has been opened, the "few" have grown to the "many," and millions there be that "go in thereat."

And the wise Lawgiver draws a very profitable conclusion following the description of the gate. The earth's Saviour then says, "Beware of false prophets, who come to you 'as wolves' in sheep's clothing." Do not fail to see the beautiful connection with what has gone before. The wolf coming in sheep's clothing has an express purpose of leading the sheep away from the place of confinement and safety. You know how, when one sheep runs in a certain direction, the many are prone to follow. The wolf comes from the wilds, the "broad" places, and moving about for a little while as a sheep among sheep, edges his way out wider and wider, that he may entice the sheep to follow him. In doing so he leads them on to the habitation of the wolves, where the words prove sadly true, the broad road leadeth unto destruction. It is so with the false prophets. They come to men, and come in the garb of friendship and of humanity. They plead against the narrow way, and sound the praises of a broader way. They say: Strike out for yourselves, why should you always let the comfort of the rest keep you from having your enjoyment. Come with me, I have been out over all the lands, and wolds, and pastures green about, and you can have a large, broad liberty. You can have your own way, and see the large life you have never seen, and never can see where you abide. There is no temptation so fascinating to man.

There is no department of human life where these false prophets do not ply their misleading craft. They appear in the pulpit and wear the garb of a Christian name, and call the Master "Lord." And yet is their plea with the sheep of Christ's flock, that they should love a way larger and broader than by the cross. That way is too narrow, too strait, too restricting, too humiliating. They have found a broader way, and a wider gate; a way unstained with the offensive blood, and unmarred with the constant sight of the repulsive gibbet. They have found a broader theology than that of Peter and Paul, and a wider hope than ever fell upon the vision of the Apocalyptic seer. And their entreaty is, "Enter ye in at the wide gate.'

And these false prophets appear upon the platform in the garb of human rights, flattering the trusting, sheep-like humanity, and scorning the idea of being kept confined by shepherds, saying, with a fascinating boast, We have a fold where we are all equal, and where there is no shepherd. Wolves have no shepherds, sure enough. Therefore, their plea with innocent sheep they make, Ours is a wild, unguided life, and we claim all fields and pastures ours, and none make laws for us. "Enter ye in at our wide gate."

And to our homes these wolves do make their treacherous way, with pleas of similar form, weaning our boys and girls away from parental influence and care. This way is too narrow, they say, and they tempt the unwary with the broader offer: Our way is a free and open one, we brook no voice of leadership from any, for we lead ourselves. "Enter ye in at our wide gate."

And so we could go on with this picture. But listen, oh! listen to the sympathetic, humanity-loving, all-knowing one, as He speaks to us all in church, or state, or home, "Beware of false prophets who come to you in sheep's clothing, but inwardly they are ravening wolves."

These, my dear hearers, are the truths which came from the pulpit of the Son of Man as He stood unfolding the kingdom of heaven to His first disciples. Are they not truths for earth? Do they not move to the very core the whole fabric of human society? Are they not for its life and for its harmony? And, in the spirit of the Divine Master, I have been striving to show to you to-night that the pulpit of Christianity is seeking to present to all mankind the remedy for all its ills. It stands prepared to tell you the cause of all earth's evils, and to prove to you its power to alleviate them. And it is the steady purpose of this pulpit to move in profound symyathy with the oppressed of every kind, and in profound solicitude for the elevation of the children of men to the highest possible gift in earth for their enjoyment. We shall count all things else lost that we may thoroughly know, and then freely declare the truth of earth's redemption by the law of Christ; which, believe me, believe God, is the only way, truth and life for this suffering earth, which God made, and which He will redeem. I know Christ said, "My kingdom is not of this world," neither is it. The spirit of this world is the "wolf" spirit with the "wide gate." But His kingdom is *for* this world. The worldly spirit could never save it. The establishment of the kingdom of heaven in it will "leaven the whole lump." Christ came to see it done! "And He shall see of the travail of His soul and be satisfied." His kingdom is for this world, for "God so loved the world that He gave His only begotten Son, that whosoever believeth on Him should not perish, but have everlasting life." Life everlasting! Yes, everlasting; because all destructive forces shall be removed, and all constructive forces be substituted. All working against one another and for self shall have been superseded by the royal law of love, which is the royal law of heaven. Then shall the Saviour's prayer be fulfilled, "Thy will be done on earth as it is in heaven." Then shall the law and the prophets be fulfilled, and once again the Saviour say, with the shout of triumph rather than of grief, "It is finished!" I have seen it done!

XI.

THE TRUE SOLDIER.

Preached to QUEEN'S OWN RIFLES, *Toronto.*

"For we which live are alway delivered unto death for Jesus' sake, that the life also of Jesus might be made manifest in our mortal flesh."

2 Cor. iv. 11.

THE TRUE SOLDIER.

THE circumstances which bring us together this afternoon are not the usual ones under which preacher and people meet. Ordinarily we speak from the pulpit to man as man, without any special regard to the place he may occupy in a social scale, or to the nature of his so-called secular pursuit. We speak to him as a candidate for the honors which God has set before him as man, and as an heir to an inheritance which comes to him as the seed of Abraham.

But you are before the pulpit to-day under organization, somewhat narrower than the broad plain of humanhood; and, coming in a special capacity, you seek to be addressed accordingly. I feel my inability in many respects to address you. But I claim, at this hour, one fitness. It is a fitness of thought. I am not going to preach you an old sermon plumed up with a little military uniform to it. The sermon of to-day is not only one that you shall receive, but it is one which you have given. It is no more my sermon than yours. If you had not invited me to preach to you to-day, I should never have thought, and never have known some things, which shall be yours and mine now, henceforth and for ever.

Rather a strange text we have chosen on which to reflect to-day! I say we have chosen, for I hardly like to take the responsibility for the choice. Just as soon as the message came to me arranging for this service, the text came trooping into my mind along with it, and though I did not welcome it, it stayed around and pressed itself upon me. And so I said, there must be something suitable, consistent, appropriate in it for the occasion, and I will find out what it is, and tell it, and my pleasant duty will be done. I am glad now that this service was ordered, that these beautiful words should receive more than ordinary attention.

The most of you, no doubt, have been made aware that, in the old lands and in the olden times, there was a great social difference between what were called professions and what were called trades. Professional life was considered noble, high, honorable, worthy of profound respect; while trade life was considered meaner, of lower grade, and without honor. And we have, in our more democratic days, become very impatient over such old-time conceptions and prejudices, and seek to dissipate their influence, and to destroy their force. And we are surprised beyond measure that they should be so deeply rooted, especially among the most intelligent and educated of society.

But when we come to examine the real reason for that social prejudice and wide distinction, our surprise and our impatience weaken. A little investigation soon brings to light the fact, that, to the minds of that age, a professional life was one where a man was obligated to place his duties to others first, and his own interests second; and that in trade life, a man had a right to care for his own interests first, and he could leave other people to look after themselves. Now, that was the great reason why professions were regarded as honorable, and the trades as mean and sordid. There seemed to be a kind of understood belief in a "calling" to all professional life, and an altar at the threshold of it, where men must lay down a great sacrifice to purchase the place and the honor. Commissions in the army, diplomas in the medical spheres, parchments of ordination in the priesthood of the Church, were titles to honor, but involved vows which merited them. The physician must sacrifice all right to preserve his own life, for the code of medical honor requires that, at all risks, he must use his knowledge and skill in the service of those who send for him. In like manner, a captain in the army has no right to think of his own life first. His men are in his charge, and the code of military honor requires that, at whatsoever risk to himself, he should hold them together and provide for their safety. The captain of a ship accepts the same lofty obligation. If, when his vessel is in danger, he jumps into a boat and pulls off, not caring first for the safety of those entrusted to his care, he incurs, and justly, too, a universal execration. How many are the stories of cool gallantry and true bravery we have been privileged to read or to hear where sea captains have stood on their quarter-deck and seen, first, the women and children, then the rest of the passengers, then the crew, and have saved themselves last of all, or, as has often happened, have gone down with the sinking ship? And how many kindred deeds of valor are recorded on the tented field of national defence. And all this is required by the laws of professional honor. Strictly speaking, then, the text of to-day could be literally quoted by all true-hearted professionalists, "We are alway delivered unto death for" some "sake." And that sake no less than Jesus' sake either; for it is written as the words of Jesus, the Judge of human acts, "Inasmuch as ye have done it unto the least of one of these My little ones, ye have done it unto Me."

I am glad indeed, therefore, that I can find any congruity between the true soldier life and the heroic utterance of the words chosen as a basis of address to-day.

When we study their announcement by the person writing or speaking them, they have a broad heroism about them that is worthy of our attention. He was a born Roman citizen, and in numerous places showed his high admiration for the bravery and fidelity of the Roman soldiery. His language on almost every page is full of military figures, and he it is that honors all true disciples with the name of soldiers. He always spoke as if he considered himself bound by a code of honor broad, and deep, and high as that of any centurion. He gave his fellow-disciples credit for the same. This clothed him at all times with a panoply of unusual courage. "We are alway delivered unto death." You can appreciate it. If always delivered unto death, then certainly always delivered unto anything less than death. They walked through life victors, because no man could take their lives from them. They had lain them down of themselves. They had the start of every opponent in that matter. Should interested friends persuade them to laxity of duty because of threatened stripes; they could respond, "We are alway delivered unto stripes, we took them in at the start, we have counted the cost." Did others say: Abate your zeal, lest stones be hurled upon you in inimical rage; their reply was, "We are alway delivered unto stones, we counted them in the cost." Did prisons open their ponderous and iron gates to receive them into darkness and chains; again they answer, "We are alway delivered unto prisons, they were in the list at the beginning." Did the gleaming sword wave above them, and death—grim and gaunt—stand before them, their calm was no less disturbed, for their response was still the same, "We are alway delivered unto death for Jesus' sake." And why all this? The cause is worthy. "That the life of Jesus might be made manifest in our mortal flesh." And what was this life of Jesus they would so manifest? It was the incarnate spirit of this same bravery, this same courage, this same heroism—the laying down of His life for His brethren. And that Jesus' spirit could not be manifest by any lesser sacrifice. Had threatened stripes called a halt in the march to duty, had the uplifted stone caused a palor upon the brave face, had the drawn sword called out a recantation or silenced a tongue from testifying to the truth, would the life of Jesus been manifest? Never! "If we live," said they, "our tongues shall speak, our hands shall work, our feet shall tread the messages of His love. If we die, it is all the same; our mortal bodies, our dying frames, shall testify the same spirit of Jesus the Deliverer of men." "We are alway delivered unto death for Jesus' sake, that the life," the saving life, the life of love, the constructing life, the immortal life, "of Jesus might be made manifest in our mortal flesh."

I have spoken of the honor that pertained to professions. In Paul's day the military was the leading profession. Medicine had not written its code, nor the service of the sea elaborated its law of service and honor, as we have them to-day. The increase of knowledge has opened up many other offices of trust, full as worthy as those of Paul's day, or those of the later centuries.

But our examination of this subject leads us to see that only by so much as men go into their walks of life with this great principle of self-sacrifice as an inspiration thereunto, must they seek either the honor of true men or the honor that cometh from God.

In addressing you to day as wearing the uniform of a British soldier, I must take it for granted that you carry a soldier's heart beneath it, that you only seek the honor because you have taken up the cross. There are, you know, some very sensible and honorable men who do not look with very strong sympathy upon our volunteer corps. But that is because they have only seen the sham side of it. They have seen a few lazy and chicken-hearted swells making an amusement and a pastime out of soldiering, their highest desire seeming to be in wearing a military uniform to parade before the nurse maids and children, and to be mistaken by the street pedlars and old women as patriots and heroes. Personally, at this time, I am glad that Toronto volunteers have won their honors in a more sturdy way, and that the sneering criticisms that used quite often to be heard have been put to silence by historic deeds of valor.

Speaking to you, then, as to the true soldier heart, living under the military code of honor, I can ask you, in harmony with the text to-day applied to you, For what great cause have you espoused the soldier life whenever called to exercise the same? You have linked yourselves to the national life, you have lain your life at its feet. Do you know it? Do you understand what is the difference between what is British and what is not? Have you ever thought how our national life is steeped in religion, and how our history is as religious as that of the Old Testament, or even as the New? Have you thought that to stand or fall for England's defence is to stand or fall for England's religion? Have you, who have taken to yourselves that very honorable name of the "Queen's Own," ever thought that your Queen counts not herself her own, nor her office her own? but says, in her every signature, "Victoria, by the grace of God, Queen!" She, and all the nation with her, hold that her position is but that of viceregent, God being the acknowledged King of this nation. When the insignia of our nationality is held out to view, what motto blazes forth upon it as though graven in eternal brass? "*Dieu et mon Droit.*" "God and my right," or in other words, "God, and what is right for me." When you march out to battle, or meet for your regular parade, what kind of flag is that which waves over your head? What means that Union Jack which poet sings and patriot brags in soaring and strong-winged numbers? A sign of crosses—three; St. George's, St. Andrew's, St. Patrick's, beautifully united. Three crosses, yet one cross—the cross of Jesus of Nazareth. March on, soldier of Britannia; march on, soldier of the cross. Take to yourselves the text as a tocsin, a war cry, as you enter the field, "We are alway delivered unto death for Jesus' sake."

Or do you take a somewhat narrower survey of your military duty and care? Is it from the standpoint of Canadian sons that you are led to espouse her cause and guard her institutions and her homes? Do you know what is Canada? Have you studied her history? Have you looked at the foundations of this superstructure rising before the world to such lofty proportions and such attractive form? Is our grand confederation of provinces into one Dominion from sea to sea well founded? Is its foundation safe? Are the articles of union true, just, right? Do you delight in them? Can a great and good nation be built upon them? Stand by them, live for them, die for them if needs be? Let no one lay any powder trains beneath them, or succeed to shake them in their well laid bed, or topple our rising glory to the earth. Or are they ill-founded? Is there any crumbling sandstone among the rock? Is there a flaw in the base of the structure? Guard us while we take it out and substitute the rock. Put your brave lives in the breach. Stand with your shoulder to the structure while the good is substituted for the ill. Let us build only on what is broadly human, on what is before, and above, and beyond sect, and creed, and kind; for these things shall fail. Humanity, brotherhood, equality, as far as rights are concerned, shall prevail. Let us build for permanence, and so upon foundations of eternal truth. Let us be established in righteousness on the Rock of Ages, on Him who is neither Greek nor Jew, neither Catholic nor Protestant, neither bond nor free, but who is all, all, and in all.

Now, may I be brotherly, and pass beyond the bounds of our narrower duty to-day. One word to you as men. To be true, and honorable and worthy men, the principle of soldiery is needful in every-day life. Not only when the stillness of some coming night shall be broken by the bugle call "To arms!" and the sleeping multitude be startled by the cry, "The foe, the foe is nigh!" and you are marshalled, as to-day, in uniformity of dress, and armed with fire, and ball, and steel, to move in phalanx against a marshalled enemy advanced; not only then, amid the excitement of crowds and blare of the trumpet, are your soldier's principles and your offering of life or death needed for the nation's weal. But "alway!" It is in the text to-day. Thank God for that! The nation's honor, the nation's strength, the nation's life, need in all hours and on all days a loyalty to its laws and customs. But the larger life of humanhood needs our life, even unto death, laid at its feet for service. By love we must serve one another. Let our lives be professional in the sense in which professional life wins honor and respect. Let not our life be a trade life, a slave life, a narrow life, which seeks only its own. Let us live for the race to which we belong; a race injured by sinful ways and ignorant waywardness. Let us live for the defeat of sin, for the race's sake. Let us live for the repulsion of error, for the race's sake. Let us live for the purity of social life, for the race's sake. Let us live for the help of every one less favored than ourselves. And this is "for Jesus' sake." This is that sake in which Paul and all his co-followers of the Lord Christ continued to glory, to present every man perfect, in Christ Jesus. Every man! That is the brotherhood unconfined. That is the cause to which we all belong, and to which we are either faithless or faithful, loyal or rebellious; in which we are active soldiers, or from which we are despicable deserters.

The Queen's own! The Queen is God's own by her own signature. Are ye God's own, too? If real, true soldiers, yes! If real, true men, yes! Settle these inquiries to day, and our meeting shall not be in vain. Amen!

XII.
A GREEK PROVERB.

"*Except a corn of wheat fall into the ground and die, it abideth alone : but if it die, it bringeth forth much fruit.*"

JOHN xii. 24.

A GREEK PROVERB.

IN the reading of our Scripture lessons this morning your attention was called to the practice of the apostle Paul in searching out the elements of truth already possessed by those to whom he was ministering; and upon these grafting the scions of that tree of life which is for the healing of the nations. We found him at Athens quoting from Grecian poets or prophets, and preaching from their texts the wonderful work of God in creation and redemption. We found him also, in his epistle to Titus, when writing about the character of the Cretans, supporting his own judgment by the sayings of "one of themselves, even a prophet of their own."

In a brief exposition of the lesson we sought to show you the correctness, and usefulness, and, indeed the almost necessity, of such a procedure. Truth, wherever found is worthy of respect and love. If, therefore, it be found sometimes where errors grow profusely round and threaten to overcome it, it must not be neglected there, but watched, and nurtured, and fed, and, by added strength given unto it, the force of the surrounding errors overcome.

In the text we study to-day we have an instance of the Saviour Himself adopting the same course. The words before us are a quotation from the Grecian, or what we might term heathen, philosophies of that day and age.

It is always valuable to know the surroundings of the Saviour when we would weigh and study His sayings. It is but a poor knowledge to be able to recite some of His utterances; for often, in our effort to apply them, we wrest them out of the environment in which they had a meaning and a potency, and place them where they become false and misleading.

On one of the few gala days in the life of Jesus here, when the multitude crowded around Him and sang Hosanna, when they marched triumphantly into Jerusalem, with the swelling chorus carried on the morning breeze, "Blessed is He that cometh in the name of the Lord," the Pharisees talked among themselves, saying, "Perceive how we prevail nothing? behold, the world is gone after Him." In recording this event, the writer goes on to say that among the multitude were certain Greeks that had come up to worship at the feast, and that they came to Philip of Bethsaida, and they desired him, saying, "Sir, we would see Jesus." Then Philip cometh and telleth Andrew, and Andrew and Philip tell Jesus.

Then Jesus spake unto them. And when He spake He made Himself known to them in their own tongue. By tongue, I mean language, or thoughts, or ideas that would be in some sense familiar or homelike to them. He first marked that hour, the hour of their approach, the hour of Jews leading Greeks to the Master's presence, as "the hour come when the Son of Man should be glorified;" when His truth should go out to all nations, and the middle wall or partition be broken down, and Jews and Greeks should be united in one fold. He then, in words very familiar to them, spake of the method by which this glory is to be realized or accomplished, emphasizing them forever by the inspiration He gave them, "Verily, I say unto you, except a corn of wheat fall into the ground and die, it abideth alone; but if it die, it bringeth forth much fruit."

In thus bringing Himself to the region of their own beliefs, He could take hold upon their mental life, and place His great mission in the midst of their great thinkings. It is as though He said, "You have often been taught the philosophy of life in a mystery; I have come to make it plain. You have said, 'We would see Jesus.' But to see Me is to see more than eye can fathom in a passing day. To see Me is really to see the life of humanity; for I am come that they might have life, and that they might have it more abundantly." To this end, according to your philosophy, which is true, I must lay down My life. I shall fail if I seek to save it. I am here to prove the truth you often hear. I die to live. 'Except a corn of wheat,'" etc.

While we are on this point, let us read along a few verses, and make note of its peculiar relation to the class of people to whom He was now speaking. (Read to the end of the 33rd verse.)

In regard to this thirty-first verse, I am disposed to endorse the view of Dr. Lightfoot, who holds that these words are understood as addressed to these believing Greeks to have the following meaning: "In a short time ye shall see what sort of a judgment this world passes. I, who am its Ruler and its Prince, shall be cast out, shall be condemned by My own creatures as an impious and wicked person. But do not be discouraged; though I be lifted up on the cross, and die like a malefactor, still will I draw all men unto Myself. The Gospel of Christ crucified shall be an agent in the hands of the Most High for the salvation of a ruined world." "I will draw all unto Me." Not only all men (the word *men* is supplied), but all things.

This is also a Grecian phrase. You know the ancients fabled that Jupiter had a chain of gold which at any time he could let down from heaven, and by it draw all the earth and its inhabitants to himself. Some of you students will be familiar with the passage in Homer's "Iliad" to this effect:

> "Now, prove me, let me down the golden chain
> From heaven, and pull at its inferior links
> Both goddesses and gods; but me your king
> Supreme in wisdom, ye shall never draw
> To earth from heaven, strive with me as you may.
> But I, if willing to exert my power,
> The earth itself, the sea itself, and you
> Will lift with ease together, and will wind
> The chain around the spiry summit sharp
> Of the Olympian, that all things upheaved
> Shall hang in the mid heaven, so much am I
> Alone, superior both to gods and men."

Dr. Clarke says that by this chain the poets pointed out the union between heaven and earth, or, in other words, the government of the universe by the extensive chain of causes and effects. He says, also, that it was probably in allusion to this that our Lord spake the words referred to above. And when it is objected that it is inconsistent with the gravity of the subject and with the dignity of our Lord that He should allude to the fable of a heathen poet, among other words he says, "It is no more inconsistent with the gravity of the subject and His own dignity for our Lord to allude to Homer, than it was for St. Paul to quote Aratus, and Cleanthes, and Epimenedes, for he spake by the same spirit."

And, now, it is a comforting thought that Jesus the Saviour of all men should come to the life, and experience, and thoughts of all its classes. In becoming God incarnate, it cannot be supposed that He came only to meet the ideas, or longings, or prayers, or expectations of the Jews, but of all mankind. If He is to be the Son of Man and the Saviour of all, He must somehow touch all in their earthly lot. He must be, as He really is, "neither Greek nor Jew" only, "Barbarian nor Scythian" only, "bond nor free" only; He must be " all, and in all."

Coming, then, to study the truth of this text, we come on a broad human basis. The great principle is couched in a saying which is not hard to be understood by any of earth's sojourners who eat and drink, sow and reap, gather into storehouse and barn, and are governed by all the regularities of seed-time and harvest. Surely we can learn this lesson to-day. It is our Lord and Saviour coming to our knowledge, to explain the sublime mystery of His life and death on our behalf. Our hope is in it. Our redemption is in it. All, all we have and are in possibility lies couched in this lesson of the Teacher who "spake as never man spake."

Our Lord compares Himself to a grain of wheat. His humiliation and death He likens to the grain sown in the ground, which grain thus decomposing brings forth abundant fruit. The "great mystery" of Christ's earthly experience, His chiefest apostle admits, and all His followers have been obligated to the same acknowledgment. To-day we credit it, we accept it, we believe it without, it may be, being able to comprehend it. Yet we are not to abandon it as a fruitless source of truth. It can be known. His devoted follower was determined to pursue any path of life that he might know Him, and the "fellowship" or meaning "of His sufferings and the power of His resurrection." But, until it is attained by experience, by a persistent and devoted following, by a drinking of His cup and a being baptized with His baptism, it must ever remain a mystery. Only the Spirit, fully possessed, can make it known. "Eye hath not seen, nor ear heard, neither hath it entered into the heart of man, these things, ... but God hath revealed them by His Spirit."

We can study the acknowledged mystery of the incarnate life of Christ, as we can study the mysterious life of the seeds and the soil. But while our knowledge is ever so incomplete, our faith, our belief, may be absolutey reasonable, and quite in accord with the highest wisdom. The greatest student of earth's phenomena cannot tell how one grain becomes thirty or sixty, how it vegetates in the earth, how air and water —its component parts—could assume such a form, emit such odors, or produce such tastes. The wisest of all earth's teachers cannot tell us how the bodies of animals are nourished by the produce of the ground; how wheat, for instance, is assimilated to the very nature of the bodies that receive it, and how it becomes flesh, blood, nerves, sinews, bones, all so beautifully and usefully related to each other.

But we know that these things are so; and we so believe in them as to lay all our plans of life upon the belief, and prove our faith well founded. And by study and devotion to this line of scientific truth man learns very much about these things. He learns truths which aid him largely in the production of fruit from the seed. He learns much of the laws of vegetation, which aids him to increase the beauty and variety of plants, and fruits, and grasses, and flowers.

So is it also with the spiritual laws which lie back of the incarnation, and life, and death of Jesus Christ our Lord and Saviour. It is a secret, indeed, to those who gaze upon it from without; but it does become more or less known to "them that fear Him." When God in His eternal purpose was carrying this great thought in His own mind and waiting the "fulness of time" when He could make it known to man; He seized one day what seemed an opportunity of telling it to the "pattern of the believers." "Shall I hide from My servant Abraham the thing that I do?" "Take now thy son, thine only son Isaac, and go and offer him a sacrifice on the mountain side." Know what I, the world's Father, will do; it can only be known by experience.

Our work in this pulpit is honest, practical work. We seek the truth for you, for your life's sake. We would lead you to know the will of God in the redemption of all those capacities and powers which in their marvellous possibilities are called your life. Consider deeply then the apostle and high priest of our profession, Jesus Christ as He is here presented seeking the harvest of ransomed humanity. The law of reproduction in the world of sowing and reaping is clear. You have all learned that the only way to an abundance of fruit is in the dying of the seed-corn. He would teach us to-day that the law of spiritual life, and power, and fruition is the same; and that it is so unalterable and inviolable that He Himself must bow to it to reach the end desired.

And following on His own submission to its stern, yet just demands, He seeks to impress it upon His disciples that, "if any man will come after Him," walk in His footsteps, be with Him where He is, and sit with Him on His throne, he too must "deny himself, take up his cross and follow Him." It is not easy. In the context we have a record of His own struggle with self. "Now is my soul troubled, and what shall I say—Father, save me from this hour? But for this cause came I unto this hour, Father, glorify Thy name." The hour is come when the Son of Man shall be—humiliated? Yes, but not finally. Glorified? Yes, but how? "Except a corn of wheat fall into the ground and die, it abideth alone;" I cannot abide alone! "but if it die it bringeth forth much fruit." For this cause came I unto this hour.

"There shall be a handful of corn in the top of the mountains, the fruit thereof shall shake like Lebanon, and they of the city shall flourish like grass of the earth. In His name shall the righteous flourish; all men shall be blessed in Him; yea, all nations shall call Him blessed."

We shall now look at the fact of Christ's submission to this law. As we have never wrought out the mystery of the corn of wheat, but have seen it a thousand times tried and proven, and so have come to believe it firmly, mysterious though it be; so must we come to the great truth it is here used to illustrate.

We must travel back in our imagination to that ancient time in that distant land of song and story. In company with a few other seekers, heaven directed, we find the humble village and reach the lowly inn. We stand around the manger cradle and lend the homage of our hearts to that of the shepherds who came to view the Saviour newly born and worship Him. Behold the unconscious infant come to bless mankind. A corn of wheat in its greenest tenderness! Behold within those swaddling clothes the chosen one of God, who is to do so much toward removing the sorrows and sins of our world. No array of splendor or of kingly pomp, no royal retinue surround Him to proclaim afar the glorious coming of the long looked for and expected One. Amid poverty and desertion, in the humblest refuge His advent is made, and

"Low lies His head with the beasts of the stall."

And yet—and yet—the child of this humility is the hope of the ages. A corn of wheat! About the manger in which He sleeps cluster the destinies of nations, and over His baby brow hangs the authentic crown of Saviour. There, on the night of His birth, and in His lowly cradle, wrapt in his peaceful slumber, we will not wake Him. Hush! Come, we will leave Him with His mother now.

Let thirty years pass quickly by without our present notice. The day has dawned upon the city of Jerusalem. It is the festival of the tribes of Israel, and nearly all have gone up to the holy place. But even more than usual stir seems to possess the multitude which throng the streets, and now move toward the city's western gate. Ah! see the vast crowd that hurry boisterously up that rising ground. Hear the hoarse mutterings that come on every side, and hark to the fiercer cry which shrieks above the common jargon: "Crucify Him! Crucify Him!" And then, behold, in the midst of the throng we catch a glimpse of His sacred form bearing His cross. Yes, it is He!

The drama is nearly over. He has accomplished the work given Him to do. It is only left for Him to drain one bitter cup, and that is at His lips. They have smitten and scourged Him. In cruel mockery they have crowned Him with thorns. They nail Him now upon the cross, and lift it, taunting Him with bitter jeers. "Oh, Thou that destroyest the temple, and buildest it again, come down from the cross." With a forgiving love unconquerable as God's, He prays for them, and His spotless spirit is in the bosom of His Father. His murderers shrink back in awe and steal away from the scene. But before we go we must meditate awhile, review His labors of life and estimate their results.

"Consider Him," as the apostle says, "who endured such contradiction of sinners against Himself!"

He has devoted Himself for all His life, and with all His energies to reveal and establish the kingdom of truth. He has manifested the perfectness of the Father, He has illustrated the true worship of indwelling love, He has taught the fulfilment and end of the ceremonial code in obedience to the eternal verities of the moral law. And whatever His lips have uttered, His character and life have enforced. But all in vain. The light of His revelation has "shone in darkness, and the darkness comprehended it not." The wise philosopher, the cold sceptic, the formal Pharisee, the haughty Sadducee, the bigoted Scribe, have sneered at His doctrine, despised His example, mocked and rejected Him. Even the chosen twelve have given Him up, lost all heart, and fled in despair, crying, "We trusted that it had been He which should have redeemed Israel." His cup of pain has been filled to the brim He has been "a man of sorrows and acquainted with grief." He had not where to lay His head. He has gone about doing good, and for the sake of His enemies has endured every pang to which innocence can be subjected. With a self-sacrifice unparalleled, He has toiled, and suffered, and wept, and prayed, and, at the last, has freely given His life-blood to establish the truth and to redeem mankind. But all apparently in vain! The brutal world, unworthy of Him, loves Him not, but hates Him, and has put Him to a violent and disgraceful death. His hopes have gone out in darkness, His life is a failure. There He hangs, a malefactor. He is dead. A friend begs the lifeless body, and carries it to a tomb. There He lies! The world is as if He had never been born, save for its fearful addition of guilt. There, they roll a stone upon the grave. "A corn of wheat fallen into the ground," and—dead.

But, if it die—what? Nay, we need wait no longer to answer this inquiry.

Pass over the years that have travelled by between that dark day and the present hour. Behold, how changed the scene! That deserted, defeated, crucified malefactor is hailed everywhere as the guide of human life. His name is above every name. He is lived for, died for, by the noblest of human hearts in every clime. In rapture His redeemed followers cry, "God forbid that I should glory, save in the cross of our Lord Jesus Christ." Oh, yes, that life, the lost life, the life of failure to human gaze, the life of that poor suffering outcast, so scourged, and mocked, and murdered for it, has won the deepest veneration, and the most profound study, and the unceasing imitation of mankind. There is no story so beloved as the record of that life. No public orator ever rehearses it without a listening auditory, no mother sings it over the pillow or her babe without tenderness, no child ever reads it without a throbbing heart, no living man peruses it with indifference, no dying man listens to it without emotion. But more still. It is the life of the poet, the inspiration of the artist, the enthusiasm of the musician. It is the basis of all philosophy now, the school, college and university critic, from which all thought and life seek to receive a commendation. All the business of modern civilization takes date from it and moves according to its calendar, as if the world only began to live when He stood upon its shores. Our cities and villages are covered with spires which are lifted in honor of His uplifting force. And beneath a million domes, or spires, or roofs, each holy Sabbath-day the multitudes of earth's best and noblest meet to study the life, and praise the name of the crucified. Asylums, hospitals, havens, associations, all for the needy, and sick, and lame, and halt and blind, cover our land as the outcome of the healing that trod the shores of the Galilean sea. Oh, "if it die it bringeth forth much fruit."

Well, ye astonished ones, it may be a mystery, but it is a fact. And we must hasten on now to mark that He who thus laid down His life that He might take it again, has asserted this to be the law of eternal life and salvation for each and all of us. He emphasized it often and strong upon those He sought to save. It used to pain the disciples to hear Jesus tell them of His own humiliation, and they could not see that the cross was the only way to the crown. But they saw it in time. "What I do thou knowest not now, but thou shalt know hereafter," was fully realized by their own submission to the same law of cross-bearing and crown-wearing. And when they came in after years to write His gracious words of life and salvation for those of us who now revel in them, how carefully they all put this one essential point of union with Him in the same mysterious law; the law of losing our life, that we may find it, of being crucified with Christ, that we might share His eternal glory.

Oh, my dear friends, we must not fail to get this idea to the full! Hear the words once more, "Except a corn of wheat fall and die, it abideth alone." If a man chooses to come after Me, let him deny himself and take up his cross and follow Me. For whosoever—it means every one of us—whosoever shall choose to save himself shall lose himself, and whosoever will lose himself for My sake shall find himself. For what shall a man be profited if he gain the whole world and pay himself as the penalty? Or, what shall a man give in exchange for himself?

In other words, Christ would have us understand that while the most glorious consequences for Himself and for others would come from His abjuring His own will in favor of that of His Father, like tremendous issues hang upon our consent or refusal to tread in His steps.

First, as to ourselves. Here we are. We have a moral choice. We can accept or refuse the path of this life and glory. No natural compulsion is laid upon us to do the will of God. We may deliberately shut all this law of divine love out of our hearts. We may eschew whatever burdens of self-denial and self-sacrifice the Christian life imposes upon us. We may seek to gain, and, therefore, lose. We may be gay, money-loving, earthly. In a word, we may follow precisely our own inclination and humor, and God will not interfere. He hath set before us life and death, and bid us choose. We shall travel on to the day of account. No lightning flash from the sky will consume us in our evil way. No spectre voice of protest, causing our blood to chill, will speak out of the darkness. On the contrary, it may go smoothly with us.

We may walk in the sunshine. We may compass all our ends. We may gain the whole world of our aspirations and desires. But there is a result inevitable. Christ tells us so. Whosoever shall choose to save himself shall lose himself. Eternal law demands it. It is in the whole realm of human life and destiny. "He shall lose himself," is Christ's very word. All the good he was made for, all the beauty and dignity of which his life on earth is capable, all the glorious potentialities of his immortal being, the very substance and soul of his God-sprung, God-destined self, he shall lose them. "Except a corn, etc., . . . alone." "But if it die . . . much fruit." Whoso shall choose to lose himself shall save himself. Oh, I cannot tell it all! You know the fulfilment of it as manifested in Jesus Christ. It is the same law in your case. and it will work you a similar achievement. "Much fruit!" The knowledge of God, which is man's highest wisdom; the favor of God, which is man's supreme blessedness; the image of God, which is man's glorious destiny and dignity; the work of God, which is man's loftiest vocation; the communion of saints in the household of God, which is man's social felicity in its purest and intensest form; the good hope of the eternal vision of God, which is man's truest consolation and sublimest prospect—this is the hundredfold fruit in the "life that now is."

And, in "that which is to come" he shall find the perfect joy of a conscious deathlessness, and shall become the possessor of all the good of which his immortal endowments render him capable; and he shall revel in the blissful, absolute, realized gain of the very substance and self of his redeemed and glorified manhood forever. "If it die, it bringeth forth much fruit."

We dare not stop here. It would be selfishness to do it. Christ had "abundant fruit," not to Himself only, but to all mankind. It was in seeking this He found His own beauty and glory. And this energy of His self-sacrificing love is called "the law of Christ." This we are called to pursue and fulfil, or fill full, in this needy world to-day.

The world is needy indeed. The sickness, the want, the intemperance, the wars, the falsehoods, the deceits, the cruelties, the desertions, the ill-requited loves, the tears that fall like rain, all go to prove and declare the great condition of suffering and need that fill the air and cloud the sunshine, and almost make the stones cry out. And now, down into this "ground" of sorrow and sin, this "seed of the kingdom" must go, to unfold again in renewed philanthropies, and increasing benevolence, and enlarged effort at removing want and lessening sickness, and mitigating severities, and reforming abuses, and securing justice, and by all ways lightening the world's burdens.

For verily, the spirit, the life of all this good is found only in the "law of Christ." It is by His spirit in the hearts of His followers He is going to lift up the fallen race. Oh, for more giving up of ourselves to the world's redemption! Friends, this is the one way to a harvest of love and joy to wave on these shores. We must be sown in the ground, given up to germinate, hidden in the dust and mire of earth's troubles and griefs, to bring forth fruit. This is what we mean when we say we are followers of Christ. This is the life that should sweeten and bless us as a Church, that should fill it with a broader charity, and a tenderer justice to all. This is the cross Christ wants us to bear. And, bearing this cross we shall dare even to go to the Gethsemanes and Calvarys of earth to suffer and die for our race. And bearing this cross we shall solve the mystery; we shall know as none else can know, the "mystery of godliness," the unspeakable joy of dying to self, and living to God.

Read this beautiful thought unfolded by a poet:

FROM DEATH TO LIFE.

Have you heard the tale of the aloe plant,
    Away in the sunny clime?
By humble growth of a hundred years
    It reaches its blooming time;
And then a wondrous bud at its crown
    Breaks out into thousand flowers :—
This floral queen, in its beauty seen,
    Is the pride of the tropical bowers.
But, the plant to the flower is a sacrifice,
For it blooms but once, and in blooming dies.

Have you further heard of this aloe plant,
    That grows in the sunny clime,
How every one of its thousand flowers
    As they droop in the blooming time,—
Is an infant plant that fastens its roots
    In the place where it falls on the ground;
And fast as they drop from the dying stem
    Grow lively and lovely around?
By dying it liveth a thousand-fold
In the young that spring from the death of the old.

Have you heard the tale of the Pelican,
    The Arab's Gimel el Bahr,
That dwells in the African solitudes
    Where the birds that live lonely are?
Have you heard how it loves its tender young,
    And cares and toils for their good;
It brings them waters from fountains afar,
    And fishes the seas for their food?
In famine it feeds them,—what love can devise!
With blood of its bosom, and feeding them, dies.

FROM DEATH TO LIFE.

Have you heard the tale they tell of the swan,
    The snow-white bird of the lake?
It noiselessly floats on the silvery wave,
    It silently sits in the brake;
For it saves its song till the end of life,
    And then in the soft still even,
'Mid the golden light of the setting sun
    It sings, as it soars into heaven;
And the blessed notes fall back from the skies,
'Tis its only song, for in singing it dies.

Have you heard these tales?—shall I tell you one
    A greater and better than all?
Have you heard of Him whom the heavens adore,
    Before whom the hosts of them fall?
How He left the choirs and anthems above
    For earth in its wailings and woes,
To suffer the shame and the pain of the cross,
    And die for the life of His foes?
O Prince of the Noble! O Sufferer Divine!
    What sorrow and sacrifice equal to Thine?

Have you heard this tale, the best of them all,
    The tale of the Holy and True?
He dies, but His life now in untold souls
    Lives on in the world anew.
His seed prevails, and is filling the earth
    As the stars fill the skies above,
He taught us to yield up the love of life
    For the sake of the Life of Love.
His death is our life, His loss is our gain,
The joy for the tear, the peace for the pain.

Now, hear these tales, ye weary and worn,
    Who for others do give up your all;
Our Saviour hath told you, the seed that would grow
    Into earth's dark bosom must fall;
Must pass from the view and die away,
    And then will the fruit appear;
The grain that seems lost in the earth below
    Will return many-fold in the ear;
By death comes life, by loss comes gain,
The joy for the tear, the peace for the pain.

XIII.

THE LORD'S BATTLE.

"And all this assembly shall know that the Lord saveth not with sword and spear; for the battle is the Lord's.

1 SAMUEL xvii. 47.

THE LORD'S BATTLE.

HOW strange are the sayings of God's servants seeking to lead men from error to truth! How they confound men with their apparent unreasonableness! "The race is not to the swift, nor the battle to the strong." How foolish an utterance! saith the experienced racer. Is not every race won by him that is swiftest; and is not the doctrine of the day the "survival of the fittest." Everywhere the great struggle is for power, power to subdue that opponent which prevents us having our way and accomplishing our desires.

Life is never pictured in truer colors than when it is portrayed as a battle-field. I have no fault to find with toy swords and toy soldiers for children, if the true lesson only accompanies the play. I have no objection to "Jack the Giant Killer" in the Sunday-school library, provided the moral leads the mind of the reader to the true conflict that must inevitably find its place in every life, and shows the youth the way to insure the victory. There are veteran soldiers before me to-day—and every Sunday—veterans of many a battle-field; some where the humiliation of defeat was their portion, others where the joy of triumph was their delight.

All grandfathers have a place upon their knee for their children's children to sit, and hear the stories which a long and chequered history so easily supplies. All have met their giants in the way. All have had the struggle with them. And the true value of grandfather's story is to help prepare the little ones for the inevitable conflict which awaiteth them.

We are led this morning to study our lesson in the valley of Elah, between two mountains, about twelve or fifteen miles from Jerusalem. Here the Philistines, those everlasting, undying, perpetually tormenting enemies of the children of Israel, are seen on one hill top, and the armies of Israel upon the opposite one. And here also a stalking giant, the chosen champion of the Philistines, is heard calling in bragging and blatant voice for an Israelite to face him in the field. He contemptuously calls Israel "Saul's servants," and declares with insulting boast, "I defy the armies of Israel this day." As we thus stand with our sympathies all upon the side of Israel, and our respect and adoration of their

God alive within us, we become very jealous for the Lord of Hosts and for His holy name.

For forty days the pompous son of Anak renews his provoking challenge; each time growing more proud and haughty because no one seems ready to go forth and meet him. Saul, renowned warrior as he was, dares not to accept the defiant offer. Jonathan, who had once attacked a Philistine outpost right bravely, and had slain ten men with his own hand, he stands back abashed before the foe.

The suspense is terrible. Like the disciples in the midst of contending waves, we would fain cry out, Master, Lord, Jehovah, "Carest Thou not that we perish?" Oh, for a Moses to plead for the honor of God's name with a perseverance that taketh the kingdom of God by force!

But our difficulty is not a difficulty with God. While the "heathen rage and the people imagine vain things," while the "kings of the earth set themselves, and rulers take counsel together," while the proud animal struts about upon the dust of which he is made, and the creature pompously defies the Creator, while the abnormal bigness—conscious after all that there is no safety in bigness—binds on the plated mail and links of rugged brass, and arms himself with shield, and sword, and spear, then to assert his almightiness over all flesh, "He that sitteth in the heavens shall laugh, the Lord shall have them in derision."

Oh, how common to us has become that saying, "Man's extremity is God's opportunity!" See! The ranks of Israel's host divide. Thence cometh forth a shepherd boy just fresh from Jesse's field. He brings —a pouch, a sling, a simple face, a firm, unfaltering step. On toward the boastful giant this ruddy shepherd draws. Goliath speaks. Vain words, of course, are his, "Am I a dog, that thus thou comest out to me?" Come on, then, come; to beast and bird thy flesh I soon will give; 'twill be a dainty meal, indeed, for vultures or for eagles young. Then from his gods Goliath prays a curse to fall upon the youth.

But list again, while David speaks: To me thou comest out with sword, and spear, and shield; I fear them not, nor do I brook to arm myself in such a suit. My hope is not in these. In my own name I come not; nor do I deign to count my strength enough to vie with thee in human fray. But thou hast once too oft defied our God and all His host. To show thee, then, that His high power abides in infinite degree, the weakest of His servants, I, He sends to hush thy haughty noise and lay thy boasted greatness low in the dust from whence it came; that all—His own and not His own—may know that in the camp of Israel still, there is a God.

Words cease. The time for deeds has come. From the rude pouch, a stone—a choice, smooth stone—the shepherd takes and lodges in the faithful sling, which many a time before in lesser dangers, it had proved itself. Then, in the simple confidence which comes always to him who hath a "single eye," and whose "body is," therefore, "full of light," he looks out at the spot whither he wills the stone should go, and hurls it in that truth of thought and truth of purpose straight to the fatal place. The deed is done. As falls the lightning-stricken tree crashing to forest floor, so falls the monster who, but just a brief moment ago, did spread himself as a "green bay-tree," but now is spread in death upon the earth, proving the wise man's words to all addressed, "Pride goeth before destruction, and a haughty spirit before a fall."

"And all this assembly shall know that the Lord saveth not with sword and spear, for the battle is the Lord's."

To every one of you the events connected with this incident are familiar. From the days of boyhood you call them up, if you have not read them this score of years or more. I have a confession to make this day which others, too, perhaps, will make with me. I have not sought to know the meaning of this recorded battle and victory since I grew to manhood's years. It has never been much more to me than a story for boys; I ask forgiveness now for my rude estimate of a kindly revelation. And I thank the Divine Spirit for guiding my thought to the threshold of its inspiring lessons to-day, and with you I pray that it may lead us to a knowledge beyond what we have ever possessed of the "victory which overcometh the world, even our faith."

First, let us take the incident apart from any relation it may bear to other conflicts. It is worth while to know the main points in the victory. To know how David came to present himself, and how he came to prevail is worth a thought for any of us. To know how Goliath, so well armed and so confident, should have so utterly failed, may be valuable to any whose faith may be like his.

Evidently, this was a conflict between two, equally confident of success. No one can say that Goliath had not as much faith as David. If it were only a matter of mental attitude, each should have been an equal match for the other. If it were a matter of means as well as faith, Goliath had evidently the advantage. Where, then, was the weakness of the big one, and where was the strength of the little one?

Goliath's faith was strong, but the object of it was weak. His faith was entirely in himself. But grant that; was not he himself strong? Yes, but faith is no use as an instrument, except it brings strength from without. Goliath's faith added nothing to his strength. If it was a very lively faith, it would tend to overestimate the strength and, therefore, misguide in action. It is thus that self-confidence withdraws attention from the value of others. It fails to take cognizance of the real strength of opponents. It is falsifying. It has no vision of truth. And, moreover, it has no elevating power. It is like a man trying to lift himself up with his own hands. To uplift ourselves we must take hold of some person or thing above ourselves. There is a philosophy of failure in pride and arrogance, which are two of the things which wisdom says, "I hate."

And where was David's strength? He had equal confidence or faith with Goliath. Wherein then did he surpass him? In the object of his faith. His faith went out and took hold upon a higher power. He was, therefore, more than himself. He was measurably more, by so much as the object of his faith was above him. His faith was in God. You know, then, the measure of his power. But how came he to have such faith in God? Where did he get it and how? He acquired it in a lawful manner—a manner open to all the children of God. First, he had nothing but the honor of God in his heart. He viewed the whole matter as a simple, innocent child of God. The challenge he heard was a challenge against God. He knew nothing as separate or distinct from God. And he felt confident that God would be with and bless any one at all who should go out in His name against the foe of Israel. And if any one, then, of course, himself. He would have been satisfied if any other had gone forth and saved the honor of the Lord. He sought no honor for himself. It was not his battle, and, therefore, it would not be his funeral, if there was one. He had no double vision, no faltering or divided purpose. He was true; he saw truly, for his heart was pure. He did not ask God to do anything for him. The affair was not for him. His faith was not an asking faith, it was a giving faith. The faith that gives is the big faith. He said, "Let me be Thy servant, Lord; let me answer him in Thy name." This was David's strength. He sought no other.

And yet, even David must be tried before he can enter so important a conquest. Mark the test to which he was subjected.

When he was inquiring from his elder brother how it was that this proud Philistine should be permitted to defy all Israel day after day, and when he displayed some sign of his own willingness to assume the responsibility, his brother taunted him. It is said that the brother was angry with him, and replied, "Why comest

THE LORD'S BATTLE. 271

thou hither? . . . . I know thy pride and the haughtiness of thy heart," and other such severe and malicious words. And that was very hard to bear. To be thus insulted in the presence of others, to have the very vilest construction put upon his motives, and all by his own brother Eliab, was a sore trial, indeed. David knew his own heart, knew that he harbored no evil purpose, knew that he had in view only the glory of God; and the attitude of Eliab stirred up a hot contest within. What shall he say in response? How shall he resent the foul, false misrepresentation? Here is a giant now stalking out upon his own battle-field. What shall be the issue in *this* conflict? Can he rule his own spirit? We do not see the inward fray. But we see the result which follows. Yes, he meekly, patiently, quietly responds to his brother, "What have I done? Is there not cause for me asking the question I did?" The hot anger of Eliab did not kindle a flame of vengeance in David's heart. "He that ruleth his own spirit is better than he that taketh a city." David's meekness wins. He rules his own spirit. He can rule anywhere. He is a victor already. He moves forward—the proven one. God intends that David shall win now; hence, he cannot fail. Had he fallen before Eliab, he could never have faced Goliath with success.

Let us now see the meaning of this divinely recorded incident to us in our day and age. That scene which we have beheld in the Elah valley long years ago, finds its constant reproduction in our world and life. David and Goliath are always with us. Here they are to-day. There is proud, self-reliant, self-sufficient strength, the big hard muscle, the tremendous bulk, the gigantic armor of the Philistine, on the one side. And there, on the other, is the slight, weak Judean youth, with nothing but a sling and stone, with his memories of struggles in which he has had no strength but the strength of God, and has conquered; with no boast, nothing but a prayer on his lips and a simple trust in his heart. We say, these two figures appear everywhere. They are confronting one another in every valley of Elah and all over the earth to-day; the power of confident strength, and the power of conscious weakness trusting in God.

And it is a battle in which all the hearts of heaven and earth are interested. Principalities and powers watch it from the upper hills, ready to shout the victory to the honor of the name they adore. And about us on every hand the vast multitude of earth's anxious sons and daughters are eager to know the issue of this unceasing noise of war. "Seeing, then, that we are compassed about with so great a cloud of witnesses," with hearts beating fast to know what is our faith and its reward, let the importance of our lesson widen, and deepen, and heighten beyond all former experience. Surely God hath not brought us to study this scene of victory for nought. Stand forth and view with honest vision the enemy upon the nether hill. Goliath stalks out the champion of vice in all its forms, seeking to overthrow the armies of the living God. War, intemperance, licentiousness, greed, anarchy, despotism, worldliness, avarice, with all their complement of clinging vices, clamor their repeated challenge to the soldiers of the cross. Are they not to be overcome? If so, how can it be? We say we do believe—I do—that swords are to be beaten into ploughshares, and spears into pruning hooks. We say we believe that peace, and righteousness, and love are to be victors in this world of ours. We say we believe that licentiousness is to give place to virtue, and envy to love, and selfishness to brotherhood, and rum is to be washed from the earth by the pure waters of the crystal river. How is it all to be done? The bold and blatant atheist, the deist, the skeptic, the rationalist, the unbeliever, all the Philistine host of the Lord's enemies are there upon the hill top, with an Ingersoll stepping out upon the Elah valley, defying the children to meet him. Not armed with such armor as that wherewith he hath clothed himself, shall the champion of the Lord go forth. Many a soul has carefully armed with outside coat of mail a willing and anxious David, and sent him forth to defeat. The David of the early day would attempt no unproven weapon. No kindred arrogance, no haughty boast, no confidence in weapon will give the victory there. The meek and quiet trust in God, the anxiety only for His honor, the willingness to abide His time, and the going forth in our own naked simplicity with such weapons as we have well proven, can find any triumph there.

Have we any Davids to lead us to victory? We have Sauls enough, I think, who boast themselves in good equipment, beyond all Philistia's best can furnish. Our Sauls have urged us to match the enemy in the methods and in the sources of strength on which they depend. A very noted preacher not long ago urged upon young Church workers and young preachers to study how the world captured so many, and utilize her resources. He said, "Watch the fisherman who is catching most fish, and copy after him." In other words, he would say, I suppose, "Go to the devil, and have him teach you how to win the souls of men." It was all a mistake. He had overlooked the words of the greater Teacher, who said, "The weapons of our warfare are not carnal, but mighty," not in themselves, but "mighty through God in the pulling down of the strongholds of Satan."

If we fail, my dear ones, it is because we have other ends to serve than the honor of God, and so cannot set out with utter trust in His presence and power. Where our personal safety, or our personal honor, or our personal gain, or any lesser motive than the one we have named, strives for a place in our hearts, there is conflict within. We cannot engage in any other till that one is settled. We saw that in David. Eliab said, "You seek your own honor, your heart is haughty, I know your pride." But David secured peace within, before he went to Elah valley to meet Goliath. Many of us are just there to-day. We are having it hot enough at home, in our own hearts. We need not fear that, though, if we be faithful. Verily, God is but preparing us for the greater victory. Is some Eliab troubling you? One from whom, least of all, you would expect it. Has some near one impugned your best motives, and wounded your earnest and honest heart? It is hard, verily, to be wounded in the house of your friends. But the Lord proveth you. If your aim is the true one, bear with the misconstruction of your accuser. Keep your heart, oh, keep it safe, for out of it are the issues of life. But, peradventure, the charge of Eliab is true. Perhaps your best good is impure, adulterated, mixed up with selfishness, and you have no singleness of eye. If so, you cannot go forth.

Is this why so many of us are standing trembling at the voice of the thundering challenge of the haughty Philistine? Is this the reason why evil can go on as it will, and we have no strength to rebuke it? Is this why the battle stands still, the enemies looking each other in the face, and the armies of Israel losing courage for want of a leader to champion their cause? Then, let us set to the conquest of our own hearts. Down with the usurpers that take God's place within! Let us learn that lesson which has seemed so hard for us to learn—that lesson of meek, simple, giving, reliance upon God. Brethren, we are standing as a Church, staring at evil and wishing it was overthrown. But that will not do. If we are true and pure in ourselves, we shall see only one end—the glory of God; and we shall readily say, " Here am I, send me."

And now, I am wondering if any of our weak and timid ones can gather any help from this study to-day. How often, it may be, did David, as he kept the sheep, wish he could go forth as his brothers had done to join the army of the king! But he was young, and he was not very muscular, and would not be chosen for a soldier. And yet, where he stayed, he was faithful. It was because he was a good shepherd that he made a good champion, and afterwards a good king. "The good shepherd giveth his life for the sheep." He had done so. When the lion came, he did not flee, as would a hireling; when the bear came, he did not seek to save his own life, but the lives of the sheep. And thus he succeeded. He had been "faithful over a few things," and so he was made a "ruler over many things." First—the lion; next—the bear; next—his own spirit before Eliab; then the great Philistine on the plain of Elah. My weak and timid friend, be faithful where you are, your pathway is to higher honor and greater usefulness. Do well what is at your immediate hand. Don't shirk the little duty. If you are a David in the pasture, you shall be a David in the valley of Elah. Home is a good place to practice for the public field.

And I have been wondering how all our lady friends are taking this subject this morning. It savors so of carnage, and the field of military prowess, that, it may be, they find but little for themselves in the lesson. But that is a mistake, indeed. Did I not confess already that I had left the narrative behind me as only a study for boys? And fool enough I prove myself this day to have been. But where is the lesson—the inspiration, the point of sympathetic touch for the woman heart to-day? We will see. When David came forth to meet the son of Anak, the giant, it is said, "disdained him, for he was ruddy and of a fair countenance." One leading commentator says he was disdained and scorned because he looked like a woman. Doubtless this very idea is couched in the expressions, and in the sneer of Goliath. Yes, David looked like a woman, and acted and spoke much like a woman, and possessed just such armor as one would think a woman might use upon the battle-field. And I just find myself wishing that it had been a daughter of Jesse that had taken the proud boaster down. But no, it were better as it is; or we men would never have heard the last of it. It was just right. It was a womanly man, a meek, confiding, simple child of God, who went forth in His name, with no military show, nor ring of clarion, nor blare of trumpet, nor roll of drum, fit type of Him who, coming in the distant day to fell the "King of terrors and destroy the works of the devil," should "not strive, nor cry, nor lift up His voice in the streets," whose kingdom "cometh not with observation," and who taught His disciples: "Whoso receiveth not the kingdom of God as a little child, shall not enter therein," and who found in a woman's heart the greatest faith He ever found, surpassing all in Israel. "The meek shall He guide in judgment, and the meek shall He teach His way."

And now let me introduce to you before I close, the

regal giant of regeneration, the Goliath of the new dispensation, the champion of the kingdom of God. He is the David of old grown up, and made valiant for all the armies of the living God. He has acquired an armor now, and He has "proven" it, too. It is not like the Philistine's armor, put on from without. It is an armor that has grown out upon him from within, and is a perfect fit for the man. It has invulnerable quality, and cannot be overcome. Like the tall son of Anak, He is girt about the loins, but not with greaves of brass; He has a breast-plate, but not of mail; He has a helmet, but not of brazen surface; and a sword, but not of polished steel. Look upon Him! He is the example for us all; and His accoutrements are furnished to every soldier of the Cross who will cultivate them. He is the hero of the day of the Lord, for before Him not one can stand. He is the one to whom all things are possible. He stands forth resplendent in His spiritual beauty, and greatness, and glory, having His "loins girt about with truth, His feet shod with the preparation of the gospel of peace, with the shield of faith, and the helmet of salvation, and the sword of the Spirit, which is the word of the Lord."

This is God's chosen victor for the conquests of the kingdom. The meekest can find the way to this achievement, and the armor can be proven day by day.

Let us all unfold, then, these spiritual weapons, and be ready for conflict and victory. Let us scorn the carnal and fleshly armor, and cherish those that are " mighty through God to the pulling down of the strongholds of Satan ;" that all the universe "may know that the Lord saveth, not with sword and spear, for the battle is the Lord's."

XIV.

THE APOCALYPTIC APPEARANCE.

"And I turned to see the voice that spake with me. And being turned, I saw seven golden candlesticks; and in the midst of the seven candlesticks one like unto the Son of man, clothed with a garment down to the foot, and girt about the paps with a golden girdle. His head and His hairs were white like wool, as white as snow; and His eyes were as a flame of fire; and His feet like unto fine brass, as if they burned in a furnace; and His voice as the sound of many waters. And He had in His right hand seven stars: and out of His mouth went a sharp twoedged sword: and His countenance was as the sun shineth in his strength. And when I saw Him, I fell at His feet as dead. And He laid His right hand upon me, saying unto me, Fear not; I am the first and the last: I am He that liveth, and was dead; and, behold, I am alive for evermore, Amen; and have the keys of hell and of death. Write the things which thou hast seen, and the things which are, and the things which shall be hereafter; the mystery of the seven stars which thou sawest in My right hand, and the seven golden candlesticks. The seven stars are the angels of the seven churches: and the seven candlesticks which thou sawest are the seven churches."

REV. i. 12-20.

THE APOCALYPTIC APPEARANCE.

SINCE our relation of pastor and people together, we have, on other Easter occasions, studied the earthly appearance of the Lord Jesus after His burial in the tomb of Joseph, and His resurrection therefrom; and only a few Sabbaths ago we spent our morning hour in seeking the lessons of His ascension from the confines of this earth to the unlimited circuit of the heavens, which received Him out of our sight. On this returning Easter-day our attention has been drawn to that still further appearance, made manifest unto John the beloved, upon the lonely island of the Ægean, whither he had been banished for the kingdom of heaven's sake.

The text has been already declared in your hearing. John was worshipping "on the Lord's day"—"in the spirit"—and "he heard a voice," declaring a presence and announcing a message. He turned in the direction of the voice, and saw the personal vision described in such minute detail before us. It was an appearance of John's Lord and Master such as he had never seen before, and which, as a consequence, he was not prepared to understand. This accounts for the solemn awe which overcame him, and the prostration of which he gives a record. This overwhelming fear the blessed Lord dispersed; for, under such a spell, John could not receive the messages, nor enjoy the fellowship, nor write the things to be revealed.

And, indeed, it is much the same with our own selves. When we begin to read the precious words of this Book, this very appearance of the Lord staggers us. Nor do we allow our fear and overwhelming awe to be charmed away by the Master's words, "Fear not;" but we pursue our way forward into the recorded messages, unprepared in spirit to understand them. In this way our spirits become enshrouded with a mystery, or a mysticism, which was never intended to accompany and disqualify in any such manner the one who sets himself to read the words of this prophecy. Rather, indeed, is it openly declared in the third verse of this chapter, "Blessed is he that readeth, and they that hear the words of this prophecy, and keep those things which are written therein." May I not humbly entreat you all this morning, in the presence of this vision of your Lord, to "Fear not?" May I not ask you to put away from you all the prejudices of a long bewilderment, and let us seek together to know the meaning of this appearance, so different, it is true, from all former manifestations?

Let our first step be to mark the immediate bearings of this vision. It addresses itself with its messages to seven churches in Asia. There were more Christian churches than these in Asia. Galatia, and Pontus, and Cappadocia, and Phrygia, and Pamphylia, all had Christian churches established in them. It is, therefore, natural to ask: Why are these seven made the objects of such special notice, and why are they mentioned in the particular order in which they occur? The answer to this question is interesting. The beloved apostle John was banished from his work, and was doubtless fretting over his charge, which consisted of these seven churches. He visited them, it is likely, in the very order they are here mentioned. Any one examining the map will see that this would be the direct circuit route. John resided for the most part at Ephesus; and, moving northward would come to Smyrna, still northward to Pergamos, then south eastward to Thyatira, and then farther south to Sardis and Philadelphia, and Laodicea, from which place a short northwesterly journey would bring him back to Ephesus again. As the metropolitan, or bishop, of the seven churches, he visited them all often, and doubtless took this most direct course, which is indicated on the map, and with which the order mentioned in the text is in perfect harmony.

And now, as we look a little closer into the surroundings of this vision, we shall find that not only had this appearance and the accompanying message a direct bearing upon these individual churches, but, indeed, that the special features of that appearance had a distinct relation to certain special features of the churches.

The object of our study this morning is the Lord's appearance as here set before us by the apostle. There are two ways in which it could be approached—the one by following the order of the vision and tracing its meaning in application to the churches; the other, by following the order of the churches. In either of these ways the same end will be reached; and the interesting fact will be learned that each church was addressed from some detail of the glorious appearance especially adapted to its own circumstances and conditions.

It will, perhaps, be slightly more convenient to follow the order of the churches.

The first church addressed is Ephesus. To this church the apostle is bidden write: "These things saith He that holdeth the seven stars in His right hand, and walketh in the midst of the seven golden candlesticks."

This feature of the appearance has its distinct value in its relation to that church. It is already recorded in the twentieth verse that, "the seven stars are the seven angels of the seven churches; and the seven candlesticks are the seven churches." The application of this will be seen in the fact that Ephesus was the metropolis of proconsular Asia, and the residence of the apostle. This church stood out as the leading church among the seven. St. John's relation to it gave it a particular advantage, a particular influence and a particular responsibility. It was first among the seven, it "walked in the midst," as it were, of the whole number. Out from it regularly went the bishop apostle upon his parochial visitations. The appearance and message of the Master was designed to indicate that as He moved among all the churches he knew their good works and their influence for good or for evil, as a representative or exemplary church. They did not, could not stand alone in the effect of their form of life, and in the power thereof. This fact is plainly brought out again, when, after many words of approval, certain counsels and reproofs are given, and a warning couched in the words "Repent, ... or else I will come unto thee quickly, and will remove thy candlestick out of his place." The promise also, which is recorded for the faithful, bears out the whole idea of this peculiar privilege of elevation and its responsibility : "To him that overcometh will I give to eat of the tree of life, which is in the midst of the paradise of God." Here the prominent place among the trees of God's garden is the prize set before the faithful. To partake of that tree which is in the midst of all other trees is the legitimate outcome of fidelity in a position of similar responsibility in the days of trial here below. To be a faithful leader in that which is least will win a leader's place in that which is most.

The next church which is addressed is that of Smyrna. Here you will notice the Lord writes under a very different signature. "These things saith the First and the Last, which was dead and is alive." The "angel" of this church was Polycarp, a disciple of St. John, and by him appointed to the pastorate. He died —a glorious martyr for the truth—at this same Smyrna, being, as he was, eighty-six years old. And now, by reading the message to this church, we can readily see that it had fallen upon times of great persecution. Death stared them in the face on every side. The whole purport of the address is to encourage the church to meet confidently the fiery trials of martyrdom in the sure hope of triumphing over death. So needy were they of comfort and succor, that the message contained no reference to any fault such as were charged against the others, but only words of a loving cheer. How beautifully becoming the signature under which it was written: I am "the First and the Last— the Alpha and the Omega, which was dead and is alive." The "First and the Last;" no one can get the start of Me, and no one can follow up my tracks. "Fear none of those things, therefore, which thou shalt suffer;" they are all within the scope of My power to direct to your glory. "I am He that was put to death," as you may be; and "behold I am alive for evermore." "Be ye faithful"—faithful unto death, and I will crown you with a similar everlasting life, for "he that overcometh shall not be hurt of the second death." In the case of this Smyrna church the application is very plain, even from the simple letter of the message. It becomes exceedingly so, as the facts of history lend their light to the scene of the church's labors and trials.

The next mentioned church is the one in Pergamos. The signature of the Lord here changes again. "These things, saith He which hath the sharp sword with two edges." We might almost forecast the message here to be one largely of reproof. Being not very far from Smyrna, the persecutions and trials referred to there had shown themselves in this community. And there were some faithful ones to be commended in the first words of the address, and by whom the "sharp sword with two edges" would be looked upon as a weapon of defence and deliverance on their behalf. But there are heavy charges against church members here. Fellowship with idolaters, with all its concomitant evils, and the doctrine of the Nicolaitanes, so hateful to Christ, were the sins charged against them. The "sharp sword with two edges" was an appropriate signature under which to write to this people. Hence the warning of the message: "Repent, or else I will come unto thee quickly, and will fight against them with the sword of My mouth." In this case, the rewards "to him that overcometh" are based upon the form of the difficulties to be overcome. Surmounting the temptation so freely besetting them to "eat things sacrificed unto idols," the promise was, "I will give them to eat of the hidden manna." Holding fast to Christ's name in spite of the martyrdom that fell upon Antipas; refusing to choose for themselves another name which would save them from enemies, and secure to them life, the promise was: "I will give them a white stone, and a new name written, which no man knoweth saving he that receiveth it."

The next church in the list is the one at Thyatira. Here is another new signature. "These things, saith the Son of God, who hath eyes like unto a flame of fire, and His feet are like fine brass." The term "Son of God" here harmonizes with the expression in the text: "His head and His hairs were white like wool, as white as snow." Without any exception, this is accepted as indicating the "Ancient of Days," and is the representation of His eternal glory as the Son of God. His appearance to this church as one "having eyes like unto a flame of fire," would lead us to suppose at once that theirs were sins of a hidden, secret character, which only a burning, penetrating gaze could reach; and He would warn them that nothing could be curtained from His scrutiny, or walled in from His all-searching sight. And the context plainly declares this to be the real facts of the case. "Thou sufferest that woman Jezebel, which calleth herself a prophetess, to teach and seduce my servants to commit fornication," etc. Mark how all this was being done under the guise of a prophetess of God, and in this secret manner such things were conveyed into the very sanctuary of the church. In this covert way many would be led astray, which the open temptations of surrounding idolatry never could have reached. And so the Master comes to turn upon their scenes of darkness His big eyes of living, exposing flame, that they might learn the old lesson: "All things are naked and open unto the eyes of Him with whom we have to do." The application of the other feature of the appearance—" feet like unto fine brass, as if they burned in a furnace," is found in the fury with which He declares He will trample upon this evil. His words are those of one who stamps with rage. " Behold, I will cast her into a bed, and them that commit adultery with her into great tribulation, ... and I will kill her children with death, and all the churches shall know that I am He that searcheth the reins and hearts ; and I will give to every one of you according to your works." The reward to the faithful, who have not known the " depths of Satan as they speak," is one of power to put this evil down, and rule these evil doers " with a rod of iron, and break them in pieces as a potter's vessel." And beside the power to suppress this evil, they should come out from the darkness of their hellish night—their light should " rise in obscurity "— they should come forth into the dawn of a new day, receiving the promise, " I will give him the morning star," *i.e.*, the star which precedes the rising of the sun, and is the first harbinger of coming day.

And now we come to the message for the church in Sardis. Here, we must admit, the relation between the vision and the message is not quite so legible upon the surface as in the cases which we have thus far studied. But, as we have satisfied ourselves already that we have found the key of interpretation for the appearance under review, it will be worth our while to give a little search for the connections in this particular instance. The signature here is: "He that hath the seven spirits of God and the seven stars." There can be no doubt that John saw the "seven spirits before the throne" as a part of his vision. In the fourth verse he makes important reference to it. His greeting is couched in the terms, "Grace be unto you and peace from Him which is, and was, and is to come, and from the seven spirits which are before His throne." Then, where reference is made to the appearance in the thirteenth verse, He is represented as clothed in the garments of a high priest. Now, if mention had been made of that in connection with this Sardis church, it would have completed the whole application of the picture. It is, however, doubtless as a high priest among the spirits before the throne, and among the messengers or angels of the church below, that He sets Himself before this people. It was the duty of the high priest of early Israel to register the living and the dead. He enrolled the names upon the record; and he "blotted out" the name from the "book of the living" when death had removed a member from the congregation of the Lord. As such, then, he approaches the church of Sardis with the charge: "I know that thou hast a name, that thou livest, and art dead." And such a state of things could not be permitted to remain. The priest was responsible for a correct record. Either the dead must be renewed to life, or the names must be erased. This gives emphasis to the command: "Be watchful and strengthen the things which are ready to die." In the reward to the faithful ones, reference is made to the garments common to Himself and them, as well as to the office of registrar, to which our attention has been called already. "Thou hast a few names which have not defiled their garments; they shall walk with me in white," and "he that overcometh shall be clothed in white raiment, and I will not blot out his name out of the book of life, but I will confess his name before My Father and before His angels."

In order of sequence we come now to study the church of Philadelphia and its message. To these the Lord announces Himself more in character than in appearance. "These things saith He that is holy, He that is true, He that hath the key of David, He that openeth and no man shutteth, He that shutteth and no man openeth." No words of reproof are found in this message. The presence of a synagogue of Hellenizing Jews there led them to a conflict upon the question as to who were the true followers of David. It was a conflict between the letter and the spirit, between the form and the power, between that which is "holy and true" and that which is traditional and characterless. The Hellenistic Jews would naturally claim that they possessed the only legitimate way into the kingdom of Jehovah; that they possessed, by the way of the prophets and the fathers, the keys of the city of David, the new Jerusalem to come. Hence the appearance of the Lord was as the son of David sitting upon His throne, not by the letter but by the spirit of holiness and truth. The patience and perseverance of the little Christian church against the Jewish pretences and asserted prerogatives, the Lord commended; and for this express reason set Himself before them as holding the key of David, opening and shutting at will. Before them He had "set the open door." Those of the synagogue of Satan who say they are Jews and are not, but do lie, He will make to come and worship at the feet of His church here. His exhortation is: "Hold fast to what you have, and let no man take your crown." The reward to the faithful is beautifully significant. Contending for a claim to the privileges of the kingdom of David and to a place in the church of the first-born, and to a heritage in the new Jerusalem, the words come with a welcome significance: "Him that overcometh will I make a pillar in the temple of my God, and he shall go no more out; and I will write upon him the name of my God, and the name of the city of my God, which is New Jerusalem which cometh down out of heaven from my God."

It is worthy of mention that this church held fast to what it had, that the crown for which it contended was never lost, that it was made a pillar—built up in the temple of God, that it has never been taken out, that it has to-day and has always had a worshipping Christian people there, and moreover that the very name of the modern town occupying the location of the ancient Philadelphia is Allah Shehr, meaning the city of God. What a beautiful fulfilment of the promise: I will write upon him the name of the "City of my God."

One more church of the seven remains to be considered. It is the church at Laodicea. The words addressed are without any commendation. They are burdened with reproof, and warning and threatening, followed by an offer of grace to the penitent. The signature here is: "The amen, the faithful and true witness, the beginning of the creation of God." "The amen," and "the faithful and true witness," and the "beginning," are all words found in the chapter where John saw the vision and heard the voice of the Lord. The idea to be conveyed is plain. This church was aimless, purposeless, frivolous. It sought no crown, aspired to no eminence, possessed no ideals, and so had no work to keep it aglow with life and heat. It was self-satisfied. As a witness it amounted to nothing, for it held no truth with sufficient loyalty or love to care to witness for it. Hence the Lord came, saying, "I am the Amen," the YES, the positive "So it is" and "So be it." I am "the faithful and true witness," the first creation to that end, for "to this end was I born, and for this cause came I into the world that I might bear witness unto the truth." Ye are neither one thing nor another, neither cold nor hot, neither yes nor no, neither true witness nor false witness. I was created—born—to witness; all who are followers of Me are born to witness also. I have no part with you, because ye are neither yes nor no, cold nor hot. "I will spue thee out of My mouth." Then, with a gracious plea, He sets before them the fact that by witnessing to the truth, by having a positive work to do and end to attain, He had advanced to a throne with His Father; and He offers them the same privilege to stimulate their spiritual ambition, and stir their sluggish souls to zeal. Contented in their own acquisitions, they are represented as having shut themselves in from the without, saying: We have no need to go forth, we are full, we are happy, let us abide as we are. And in tender solicitation the Lord says: "Behold, I stand at your shut door and knock, if any man hear My voice and open the door I will come in and sup with him, and he with Me, and to him that overcometh will I grant to sit with Me upon My throne, even as I also overcame, and am set down with My Father on His throne."

And so we have seen that every feature of the awe-inspiring appearance of the blessed Lord to the beloved apostle found its place of living application in the messages which John was called to write. It must have been quite a charm to him as that form before which he trembled and fell as dead so unfolded itself to him in its true, living, spiritual import and application. Let it not be less charming to us to-day; and let us, now that we have been divested of our strangeness, make ourselves still more familiar with the vision and the words of this Book which carries in its preface a promised blessing to those who read, and hear, and obey its gracious words of life.

And now, after such a study as we have had this morning, it would be a great omission if we should overlook these words, addressed to ourselves and repeated seven times over in our short lesson: "He that hath an ear let him hear what the Spirit saith unto the churches." In every case, though Jesus the Lord is the original speaker, He does not fail to acknowledge the dispensation and work of the Holy Spirit. This only indicates their blessed unity. "He shall receive of Mine," said Christ, "and shall show it unto you." When you retire to your homes, take your Bibles and read over these messages to the churches. I have only touched upon them, and introduced the speaker unto you. A charming occupation is before you now if you will only embrace it. And by way of help you may mark three great leading forms of communication which the Spirit made to the churches.

He communicated words of commendation. Six of the churches out of the seven were commended. Bless God, in almost all churches there is good which Heaven itself looks down upon and delights in. And what things seem here worthy of the Lord's commendation? Well, emphatically, *works*. "I know thy works" was the eulogy passed upon Ephesus, and Smyrna, and Pergamos, and Thyatira, and Philadelphia. "Labor," "service," "charity," are words of commendation. And *patience* is deemed a worthy characteristic in the church. "I know," said the Spirit, "how thou hast borne, and hast patience, and for My name's sake hast labored and hast not fainted." And *progress* is commended. "I know thy works, and the last to be more than the first" is the kind word of encouragement to the church of Thyatira.

And mark, in your reading, that the Spirit speaks to the churches words of *reproof*. Departing from the first love is deemed censurable. We must not overlook this. Too many of us have the erroneous impression that the first warm, ardent, simple, sincere love cannot be retained, and that we must of necessity pass into a state of spiritual declension. Oh, no! no! Nothing is so painful as a declining love to one who loves us faithfully. And nothing is more perilous to the human heart than this loss of early love. Let us be warned from declining by the reproofs of the Spirit; and let us be glad to learn that better things are looked for by Him who loves us with an unfailing affection.

And the Spirit reproves *neglect of church discipline*. The angel of the church of Thyatira was censured as it reads: "Thou sufferest that woman to teach," etc. There is a dread responsibility in rightly keeping the purity of a church, and guarding the words that are put before the babes and children of the kingdom.

And the Spirit reproves *hypocrisy*. "Sardis had a name to live and was dead." It is said that hypocrisy in the church is a more powerful obstacle to progress than infidelity in the world. The one is a treacherous foe within the citadel; the other an open foe without.

And the Spirit reproves, with emphatic brevity and precision, *lukewarmness* in religion. The Lord declares that this, though it may not excite His fury like the evils of Jezebel, yet to Him it is unendurable. He avers, with plainest speech, that it makes Him sick.

He can hold no fellowship with such as manifest it. "I will spue thee out of My mouth" is the offensive threat to the lukewarm professor. Ponder well this utterance of the Spirit, and mark while you read that the Spirit speaks unto the churches *words of promise.* I will not break the charm that comes from counting them over. I could be a good Catholic and count these beads over every day to the good of my soul and to the glory of God. I leave them for your cheer as they point your soul upward to the most glorious acquisitions, and I pray God to charm you to a renewed zeal and energy that shall insure to each of you the reward declared to him that overcometh.

My dear fellow-disciples in the Church of Jesus Christ, we have seen the Lord to-day, not in the humiliation of His earthly pilgrimage, but in the glory of His well-earned triumph. We have learned that He forgets us not while He reigns above; but lives in anxious eagerness for our welfare in all good things. He would stimulate the good in us; He would mark with displeasure the evil and help us to put it away; He would lead us onward, upward, *homeward* to the glory of an eternal splendor, a splendor of being within, and a splendor of environment without, and consequently a harmony inviolable—the fulfilment of the promise: "Ye shall share His glory."

THE GUIDING EYE; or, The Holy Spirit's Guidance of the Believer. By Rev. A. Carman, D.D. Cloth, limp, 221 pages, 50 cents.

THE GUIDING HAND; or, Some Phases of the Religious Life of the Day. By Rev. E. A. Stafford, D.D. Cloth, limp, 189 pages, 50 cents.

THE BAPTISM OF FIRE; and Other Sermons. By Rev. J. Wesley Johnston. Cloth, bevelled boards, 201 pages, 75 cents.

SERMONS AND ADDRESSES. By the late Rev. S. J. Hunter, D.D. Cloth, 360 pages, $1.25.

THE TRANSFIGURATION OF CHRIST, and other Sermons. By the late Venerable Samuel Dunn. With a Biographical Sketch of His Life by Rev. J. Dunn Dinnick. Cloth, 266 pages, $1.00.

SELECTED SERMONS AND LECTURES. By the late Rev. Wm. Stephenson. Cloth, bevelled boards, 192 pages, 75 cents.

Post-paid at Prices Attached.

WILLIAM BRIGGS,
Wesley Buildings, Toronto.

MONTREAL: C. W. COATES.   HALIFAX: S. F. HUESTIS.

Our Own Publications.

Methodism and Anglicanism. In the Light of Scripture and History. Limp cloth, 75 cents.

Age of Creation. By Wm. J. Cassidy. Cloth, $1.25.

Antinomianism Revived. By Rev. Daniel Steele, D.D. Cloth, 75 cents.

The Class-leader. His Work and How to Do It. Cloth, 30 cents.

Immersion Proved Not to be a Scriptural Mode of Baptism. By Rev. W. A. McKay, B.A. Paper, 25 cents. Cloth, 50 cents.

Christian Baptism Illustrated. By Rev T. L. Wilkinson. Paper, 40 cents. Cloth, 60 cents.

Biblical Difficulties Dispelled. By Rev. George Sexton. Cloth, $1.00.

Light In the Cloud. By Rev. George Sexton, D.D. Cloth, 60 cents.

Loving Counsels. Being Sermons and Address. By Rev. Charles Garrett. Cloth, 75 cents.

Aggressive Christianity. By Catherine Booth. Cloth, 50 cents.

Godliness. By Catherine Booth. Cloth, 50 cents.

Tactics of Infidels. By Rev. Father Lambert. Paper, 30 cents. Cloth, 60 cents.

The Methodist Pulpit. A Collection of Sermons from Methodist Ministers in Canada. Cloth, $1.00.

The Christian Rewards. By Rev. J. S. Evans. Cloth, 30 cents.

Post-paid at prices attached.

WILLIAM BRIGGS,
Methodist Book and Publishing House,
TORONTO.

Montreal: C. W. COATES.   Halifax: S. F. HUESTIS.

www.ingramcontent.com/pod-product-compliance
Lightning Source LLC
Chambersburg PA
CBHW021955220426
43663CB00007B/829